Docks of the Mersey

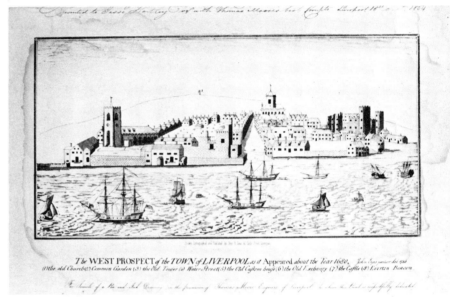

The WEST PROSPECT of the TOWN of LIVERPOOL as it Appeared about the Year 1680, John Eyes senior ad. ...
(1)the old Church (2) Common Garden (3) the Old Tower (4) Water Street (5) the Old Custom house (6) the Old Exchange (7) the Castle (8) Everton Beacon

The name of Liverpool is known world-wide. Sadly, it is now known largely for football, pop music and unemployment. Behind this lies the memory of a great port, a dominant port which in 1930 exported more British goods than its nearest five competitors combined. Memories also linger of the transatlantic liners, the cotton trade and a host of worldwide activities of greater or lesser benefit or importance. It may seem strange to explain the events which brought about this prosperity, but the medieval Mersey was such an inhospitable and inauspicious place that some explanation is necessary.

To the east of Liverpool lay a broad belt of ill-drained mosses, some parts of which were barely passable on foot, much less so with vehicles or beasts of burden, and main north/south routes steered well to the east of them. Warrington, as the lowest bridging point of the Mersey, had been of some importance since Roman times, as had Preston, Lancaster and Manchester. The roads serving these towns made a pretty effective Liverpool bypass, and some definite incentive would be needed to make people come west of them — an incentive, perhaps, like a fine navigable estuary. The Mersey, however, was no such thing. Its mouth was obstructed by a rich profusion of sandbanks, and its bottle-shaped estuary produced further hazards for the would-be mariner. Near Speke Hall, the river was over three miles wide, whilst by Birkenhead Priory it was

well under a mile. The tidal range was large, and the result of the combination of these circumstances was a fearsome current through the narrows on both ebb and flow.

On the Cheshire side of the river the picture was no more promising, for the natural problems of the river meant that any traffic which could go via the Mersey could probably go more safely by the Dee; the road layout reinforced this likelihood by funnelling traffic towards Chester. At

Birkenhead there was a small priory, which held the right to provide a ferry service across the river, but it was rather small beer by the standard of the port of Chester. Liverpool existed: Liverpool had a charter, granted by King John in 1207 to prevent his being overly dependent on the Earl of Chester for shipping facilities. There, with the exception of a few fishing boats and a tiny coastal trade, the matter ended.

It was not until the second half of the 17th century that there was any material

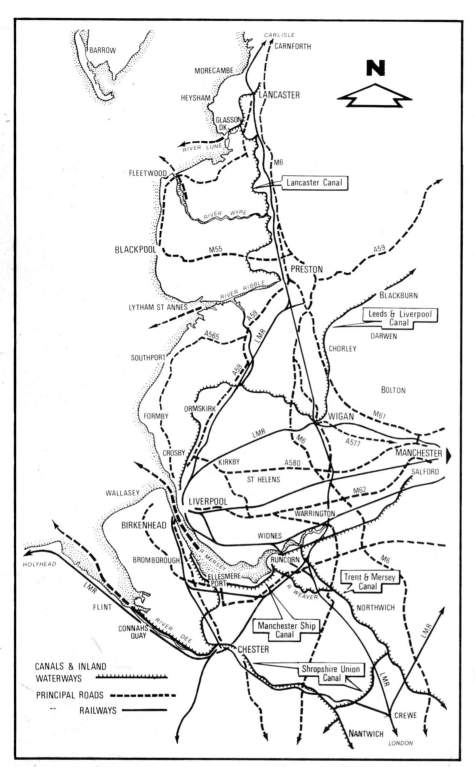

Left:
Liverpool Bay, showing municipal areas, roads, canals and railways.

change in this situation. Trade had gradually increased on the Mersey aided by the silting of the Dee and by a fairly enterprising spirit among the inhabitants of Liverpool, but by no stretch of the imagination can we see a great port in the making. In the 1670s a number of developments significant for the future occurred, though at the time they can scarcely have seemed revolutionary. North American tobacco had been coming into Liverpool since the 1640s at least, but 1670 saw a vital catalyst in the shape of the first cargo of West Indian limes. Seventeenth century ocean trading was severely hampered by the incidence of scurvy among seamen, and so the curing of the vitamin C deficiency — which was the root cause — by provision of healthy durable limes enabled an expansion of all manner of long distance trades. Equally important to the sailor (if not as conducive to his well-being) was a good supply of cheap rum, and this too appeared on the Mersey in the same year.

That same portentous year also provided an event much nearer home which would have far-reaching implications. A test-boring made in the grounds of Marbury Hall, near Northwich, provided not the coal which was sought to fuel the pans of the brine pumpers, but rock salt. The Mersey was well placed to export salt not only to Ireland and the Isle of Man, both of which lacked that vital commodity, but also to the colonies across the Atlantic which were similarly deficient. The need to bring together coal and salt was perhaps the most important of the early incentives to provide dock and harbour facilities on the estuary. Within the next century it was to prove a major factor in the development of docks not only in Liverpool and on the Weaver, but also at Garston, Runcorn and Warrington, and as it became the foundation of the infant heavy chemicals industry it was almost solely responsible for the birth of Widnes.

The first enclosed dock on the Mersey (and the first commercial enclosed wet dock in the world) was opened in Liverpool in 1715, and it rapidly became apparent that some of the problems of the inhospitable estuary could be solved in this manner. The provision of a dry dock was of immense value for long distance trading vessels: no longer did they have to carry out running repairs by the tiresome and sometimes dangerous procedure of careen-

Left:
One of Liverpool's oldest traffics (first recorded in 1648) was in tobacco. Here hogsheads are being taken out of bond at Stanley Dock for transport to one of the several tobacco works in the city. Note the vehicles: a steam lorry, a steam lorry converted as a tractor and a smart new Dyson Standard trailer. British American Tobacco still has a large works on Commercial Road. *MCM*

DOCKS OF THE
MERSEY

Produced in association with the National Museums and Galleries on Merseyside

ADRIAN JARVIS

LONDON

IAN ALLAN LTD

First published 1988

ISBN 0 7110 1533 3

Published by Ian Allan Ltd, Shepperton, Surrey; and
printed by Ian Allan Printing Ltd at their works at
Coombelands in Runnymede, England

Front cover:
An aerial view of Liverpool, 1969.
Aerofilms

Front cover, inset:
**The White Star liner *Celtic* seen off Pier
Head.** *MCM*

Back cover, top:
**The Merseyside Maritime Museum seen
from the Woodside Ferry in March 1988.**
Colin Pitcher

Back cover, bottom:
**A view of (left to right) the Liver Building,
Cunard Building and Dock Offices.** *AEJ*

This page:
**The Port of Liverpool includes deep water
berths at Gladstone and Hornby docks to
cater for 'break-bulk' and general
non-containerised cargoes.** *MD&HC*

Key to abbreviations of photo attributions
MCM National Museums & Galleries on
  Merseyside
MD&HC Mersey Docks & Harbour
  Company
AEJ Author's own
NWSIAH North Western Society for
  Industrial Archaeology & History
IAL Ian Allan Library
PoM The Port of Manchester
B&I Britain and Ireland Ferries
MPTE Merseyside Passenger Transport
  Executive

Contents

ing. The result was that the traffic grew rapidly from its small beginnings, and it was soon apparent that further dock accommodation would be necessary. In 1709 one ship, of 30 tons, was recorded as belonging to Liverpool; by 1751 there were 220, with a total tonnage of 119,175. In the same period the tonnage actually using the port more than doubled, and the population supported by this growth in trade had risen from something less than 5,000 to some 18,000. It is therefore scarcely surprising that in 1753 Salthouse Dock was opened, or that it was quickly followed by two new dry docks in 1765.

Meanwhile, elsewhere on the estuary, the stimulus of the coal/salt trade was beginning to show results. As early as 1732 the first stage of canalisation of the Weaver had been completed, though for a long time it had no terminal basins as such, as it used the natural channel of the river as far up as Frodsham. The enhanced availability of salt by water would, despite the poor initial results of the navigation's trading, encourage developments elsewhere around the estuary which in turn led to the Weaver being continually enlarged and improved over a long period.

The enabling act for the Weaver improvements had been passed in March 1721, and it was only three months later that an act enabled a similar improvement scheme involving the building of locks and new 'cuts' along the course of the Mersey from Bank Quay, Warrington, and its tributary the Irwell into Manchester. Progress on this second scheme was not so rapid: its actual opening date is uncertain, but was most likely in 1736. As in the case of the Weaver, it did not immediately provide dock installations on the Mersey, but it stimulated further growth in trade, and therefore made their eventual con-

struction very likely. This navigation was not so much concerned with the basic commodities of coal and salt as with the carrying of a variety of goods and materials to and from Manchester. It was Manchester's first reasonably reliable route to deep water and the international trade thereon.

By 1750 Liverpool was not only trading on the Mersey and beyond, but was becoming quite heavily involved in a number of manufacturing and process industries. Two of these, salt and sugar refining, were well established, while pottery and various metal-working industries were becoming so. There was an

Above left:
Widnes became a chemical boom town in the middle of the last century. Whilst it was an undoubted technological and economic leader, it must have been a vile place to live. This malodorous backwater was West Bank Dock, the site of which is now infilled and landscaped. The remains of the Mersey 'flats' *Robert Peel* and *Alice Burton* are still in there. *MCM*

Above:
One of the nicest buildings in Runcorn, Bridgewater House was built by the Duke of Bridgewater as his local headquarters while the canal was under construction. Like the canal, the house eventually passed into the ownership of the Port of Manchester. *AEJ*

Right:
Runcorn Docks: all is peaceful on Sunday morning, but the part of the docks which survives is quite prosperous. Only relatively small ships can get inside, but larger ships use the deeper berth outside. *AEJ*

arms and three new basins spreading from it.

The canal builders had by no means finished with the Mersey. The highly unsuccessful Chester & Nantwich Canal was absorbed as part of the Ellesmere Canal Co's ambitious proposal to link Mersey, Dee and Severn along routes taking in some of the most important industrial areas in the country. The connection with the Mersey involved bringing the 'Wirral line' from Chester through the Backford Gap to the river close to the village of Whitby. In 1796 the line was completed through to Chester, and it was also in that year that we find the first recorded use of the name by which we now know the place officially designated 'Whitby Locks' — Ellesmere Port.

The Ellesmere Canal Co was not destined to succeed in its grandiose endeavours, but the tiny settlement which grew around three rather isolated locks and a tidal basin was eventually to become a substantial town with a small but effective system of docks and a very large traffic on the river.

These developments around the estuary were not, as yet, in competition with Liverpool, being engaged in complementary activities. Their growth coincided with a rapid growth in Liverpool's overseas trade, with a resulting increase in population — and the building of more docks. The pace was beginning to increase, with the opening of George's Dock in 1771, King's in 1788 and Queen's in 1796. The tonnage of ships owned in the town in 1801 had reached 129,470, which represented a 675% increase over 50 years. Almost everything Liverpool touched at this period seemed to turn to gold: its success in the slave trade is well known, but even in the whaling trade, where its involvement is little known, the town was extremely (if briefly) successful. Trading expansion had been accompanied by manufacturing expansion, not only in Liverpool's now traditional industries of sugar and tobacco processing, but in machinery manufacturing, glassmaking, pottery and instrument making. In 1823 heavy inorganic chemicals (based, of course, on salt) arrived, but such by then was the prosperity of the town that it could afford literally to turn up its nose at James Muspratt — or rather at his evil fumes — and harass him out of town.

The various inland waterways mentioned above were beginning to make their impact. As the initial debts were paid off, and as trade grew, money became avail-

ever-increasing demand for coal to fire the furnaces of all these, a demand which was not being adequately supplied either by water or by the turnpike which led to the collieries at Prescot and Cronton. Matters were brought rapidly to a head by the turnpike commissioners' decision to increase charges in order to improve their road: in 1753 there were riots about the price of coal in Liverpool, and a hasty toll reduction the following month was not sufficient to stave off demands for some more radical remedy. Within six months surveyors had been engaged to investigate the possibility of canalising the Sankey Brook from near Warrington up to St Helens, where large supplies of coal could be obtained. One of the two leading promoters was John Blackburne who owned the saltworks from which Salthouse Dock derived its name, and also the saltworks at Garston (where a street adjacent to the former site of the saltworks still bears his name). Once again, the Sankey Navigation's opening in 1757 does not mark the appearance of extensive terminal docks, but the increase in activity on the river made such developments elsewhere more likely, and the time would come when the Sankey would score a rather curious 'world first'.

Precisely how and why the Duke of

Bridgewater came to build his canal is a subject which has been too controversial to allow any comment in a brief introduction such as this: suffice it to say that he built the first canal in this country to be independent of an existing watercourse and that it joined at Preston Brook with the Trent & Mersey Canal, which was the first to cross a watershed and the first to make it possible to cross Britain from coast to coast by water. The Duke's canal originally relied on coal trade, but when it was extended to Runcorn it immediately became a second (and superior) route to Manchester and also a link with other parts of the Cheshire saltfields. Above all it provided the link with the Potteries, whose supplies of clay, flints and bonemeal and whose output of pots virtually called into being a new small port overnight. Runcorn stood at the only convenient ferry point on the Mersey between Warrington (the lowest bridging point) and Birkenhead, so it is scarcely surprising that there was a village of some antiquity there, but the arrival of the Duke's canal in 1776, and the buildings of two small basins there, was the beginning of a process which was to make it probably the second largest canal port in the country (behind Goole). By 1800 the original bottom basin had developed into a strange 'inkblot' shape, with a number of able for further investment, some of which occurred at the canals' termini. Since, however, the canal companies were not trying to establish independent ports in competition with Liverpool, but merely to gain convenient access to it, we also find that they began to seek an operating base in Liverpool. The first to arrive was the Duke of Bridgewater: in 1773 he opened Duke's Dock on land he had obtained in 1768. Buildings followed, including an eight-storey warehouse which was completed in 1783, and further investment in the 1790s saw the dock itself extended.

The Duke was soon followed by a modest presence on the part of the Mersey & Irwell Navigation, when in 1784 it rented the exclusive use of a quay which was already customarily used by flats, and five years later rented the sheds, cranes and other appendages. This was followed in 1804 by a longer lease, but accommodation was still not adequate, so in 1807 the company leased the whole of the small tidal basin to the river side of George's Dock passage, with permission to convert it into a proper wet dock. Manchester Dock, which was eventually infilled in 1928, was completed by 1813. Immediately to the north, the Ellesmere Canal Co had found accommodation for its flats in the more modest shape of Chester Basin. Unimpressive though these developments were when compared with, for example, the King's Dock tobacco warehouse which was completed in 1811 with a floor area of three acres at a cost of £140,000, they were a vital part of the distributive network which turns a harbour into a port.

In Runcorn too there was activity. In 1804 the Mersey & Irwell's extension, the Runcorn & Latchford Canal, opened through to river locks and a terminal basin about a mile upstream of the Duke's docks, while downstream the Weaver Trustees were attacking the same problem of an unreliable natural channel by extending their waterway down from its old terminus at Frodsham to a river lock at Weston Point where, once more, a small wet dock was provided. Whilst, once again, the main cargoes sought were the inevitable coal and salt, it is worth remembering that in 1784 the first small cargo of North American cotton had been landed in Liverpool, forming a token

starting point for what was to become the largest trade the world had yet witnessed, and one in which the Mersey's domination was total. The Bridgewater and the Mersey & Irwell were to share in the immense wealth which this trade generated throughout the region.

Anywhere that there was a usable inlet from the Mersey might become fair game for the dock builders, and during the late 18th century the little settlement of Garston was to be no exception. In 1260 it was recorded as having a water-powered fulling mill, which might have been the first textile mill in Lancashire, but Enfield records (in 1774) that 44 different kinds of fish, including salmon and sturgeon, had recently been taken by the fishermen of Garston — that was a situation the chemical industry would soon change. The Blackburne's saltworks has already been mentioned, and would survive until 1865, but perhaps more ominous was the (albeit brief) intervention of Thomas Williams, whose Parys Mine Co dominated the copper industry during the late 18th century and is one of the most remarkable

industrial success stories of all time. His activities involved a great deal of water-borne trade on the Mersey, principally involving Liverpool and the Sankey Canal, but for some seven years he was operating a major vitriol (sulphuric acid) plant at Garston, at a time when vitriol supply was in the hands of a very few manufacturers. Presumably this was an example of vertical integration to service the brassware off-shoots of his empire, but it was to set the industrial tone of Garston as a centre for evil-smelling enterprises for a very long time to come. Each of these two under-takings had tiny tidal basins, the remains of which may still be seen today, but the birth of the 'port' of Garston had to wait a further 50 years for another example of vertical integration before it would become recognisable for what it is today.

No mention has yet been made of the effects of the Napoleonic Wars, and this is no accidental omission; in terms of the trade on the Mersey and the investment in docking facilities their effects were relatively slight. There was a certain lack of capital due to funds being diverted into

Above:
A view standing on the infill of the New Basin and looking across the entrance to Christ Church, Weston Point. In 1840 the Weaver Trustees sought and obtained Parliamentary sanction to expend surplus revenue on church accommodation and religious instruction for those who worked on the river. Christ Church was completed the following year, and the Trustees also built a parsonage, paid the minister and the choir, and provided books. *AEJ*

trading rather than building, but parliamentary activity for the enabling of new docks continued, and in 1813 Canning Dock was completed, followed in 1816-17 by Union Dock. These were comparatively small however (four acres and 2¾ acres respectively) and Liverpool's expansion seemed to get right back on course with the opening of the largest dock to date, namely Prince's, at 11⅓ acres. An apparent lull in new openings followed, but it was a lull which concealed the planning and preparation of the port's most vigorous expansion under its new engineer, Jesse Hartley. Little known and less liked by the London-centred engineering 'establishment', Hartley has only recently been

recognised for the outstanding engineer he was. Between 1824 and 1860 he stamped his personality on the port with granite walls and buildings, many of which are as sound today — and as expressive of the man — as the day they were finished. His output began to 'come on stream' with Clarence Dock in 1830, and proceeded so rapidly as to be better expressed as a list:

1832 Brunswick
1834 Waterloo
1836 Victoria
1836 Trafalgar
1845 Albert
1845 Canning Half-tide
1848 Salisbury
1848 Collingwood
1848 Stanley
1848 Nelson
1848 Bramley Moore
1849 Wellington
1849 Wellington Half-tide
1851 Sandon
1851-52 Huskisson entrance and dock
1859 Canada

The total acreage of docks built before Hartley's appointment was 46, while Hartley's output, built in just over half the time, was over 145. Nor does that total include those docks built before his long and fruitful office which had been, by his standards, inadequately built and which now bear his granite hallmark, or those docks later acquired in Birkenhead which were later brought up to standard.

Hartley's prodigious building record looks, to late 20th century eyes, like something of an ego-trip. The only sense in which that is true is that the trade of the port was sufficiently prosperous to allow him not merely to expand dock facilities, but to do so in what he considered the proper manner. As to the necessity of the expansion itself there could be no question. Cotton had been the great success story since the ending of the slave trade. In 1810 imports through Liverpool had been some 40,000 tons and by 1852 this had grown to 365,000 tons. The dominance of this huge cross-ocean trade which Liverpool achieved can perhaps best be understood by comparing the figures for other ports; London, Hull, Bristol and the Clyde ports were the 'runners up' and they *totalled* the unimpressive figure of 26,000 tons. In that same year, Liverpool's cotton merchants had £5,778,000 worth of cotton held in stock in local warehouses, and could fairly be described as controlling the market. It is normally assumed that the canals and railways serving Liverpool moved raw cotton inland and returned cotton cloths, yarns and fabrics for export, but so strong was Liverpool's hold that they also carried into Liverpool (again in 1852) a little over 4,000 bales of raw cotton brought into the country through other ports. Those other ports lacked Liverpool's storage and (more importantly) brokerage services to sell the goods. In 1851 there were over 140 cotton brokers in Liverpool, while by 1870 there were over 200.

This position of dominance may perhaps be traced to a single man. In 1784 an American ship unloaded a cargo in Liverpool which included eight bales of raw cotton. Some difficulty ensued because HM Customs, perhaps naturally, assumed that the cotton came from the West Indies like all previous imports to Liverpool. In fact it came from North America and was the beginning of the relationship between Lancashire and what may concisely, if anomalously, be termed the 'Confederate States', which would shape so much of the next century's trade on the North Atlantic. The man to whom those bales were addressed was William Rathbone, second of a Quaker dynasty of merchants to bear that name, and the effective founder of one of the most influential of Liverpool's 19th century families. Not only did he start what was to be the most dramatic new trade that even Liverpool's dramatic trading history could show, but like others of his kind he both reinvested his money in other local enterprises and took pains to use his wealth and influence to make Liverpool a better place in which to live. As an example of the former, we can probably do no better than recall his involvement in another Quaker enterprise, the Phoenix Foundry. Originally a branch of the famous Coalbrookdale Co, this firm not only used Liverpool as an exporting port for its considerable output of sugar-cane processing plant to the West Indies, but was also a leader in providing within the town that engineering infrastructure which was to help its growth.

The excesses of the subsequent stages of the French Revolution and the arrival on the scene of Napoleon, silenced Liverpudlian demands for free trade; throughout the Napoleonic Wars the issue of restriction in trading, especially with North America, continued to provoke noisy political meetings. What is significant is that both rich and poor in Liverpool had identical interests in the controversy, and it is perhaps worth recalling that had HM Government listened to William Rathbone and William Roscoe — both members of a wealthy and learned clique — it would successfully have avoided the absurd American War of 1812.

One young man who started as a junior in Rathbone's firm was James Cropper, another Quaker. He was soon successful in the American trade and, in addition to his activities as a merchant, he established the first regularly scheduled packet service between Britain and North America. He was also agent for the celebrated Black Ball Line, one of whose ships was named after him. Like Rathbone, he was something of a radical, holding a particular enthusiasm for the abolition of the trading monopolies of the East India Co and the West Africa Co.

Once a prominent anti-slaver, he moved through the other issues of the day with a similar disrespect for the status quo. In 1829 he moved a resolution at a public meeting called by the Mayor of Liverpool to consider the position of the East India Co. His seconder, who made a fiery and vitriolic speech, was Henry Booth, yet another of Liverpool's Protestant dissenting radical merchants.

There is one curious and often-noted weakness in the development of Liverpool's docks in the second half of the last century, and that is the paucity of their links with the railways. The original purpose of the Liverpool & Manchester Railway (pioneered by Cropper and Booth, it became the first railway to connect two major centres of population; it was also the first all-double-track steam-hauled railway) had been the carriage of goods, through the formation of a direct connection between Liverpool docks and the manufacturing areas in and around Manchester. In this the company did, in part, fail, in that its terminus was on the landward side of the Dock Road. The direct offloading of vessels over-side on to railway vehicles was not yet possible, and railway crossings of the Dock Road remained strangely few until almost the end of the century. Partly as a result of this, the railway was relatively much more successful in carrying passengers than

goods, and as late as the 1850s the Bridgewater Canal was still carrying substantially more cotton than any other single company. The reasons for this are unclear, for not only had Liverpool played a prominent part in bringing the railway industry into being, it continued to invest in railways and to maintain representation on the boards of major railway companies for the rest of the century. One possible reason may have been a marked and traditional distrust of anything which was not controlled from Liverpool, which went far beyond the well-known rivalry with Mancunians.

Whilst the arrival of the railways had been the source of considerable improvements in the movement of goods and passengers, it had not been quite so revolutionary as is sometimes claimed: canals and, indeed, stagecoaches, were to continue to render good service to Liverpool trade for decades yet. If we are to look for what is nowadays inelegantly styled a 'quantum leap' it is perhaps to transport in the vertical direction that we should look. Prior to 1846, the operation of cranes had progressed remarkably little

Top:
The growth of the port of Liverpool in the 19th century was so rapid that much of its early fabric was swept away. The area just south of Pier Head, known as Nova Scotia, survived into this century, and we are fortunate that a local artist preserved his view of this little 'time capsule'. Here he looks across George's Dock Passage to what one imagines had once been typical — a jumble of maritime trades, houses of refreshment and warehousing. *AEJ*

Above:
A Mersey flat off Canning Entrance. In the background are the huge Albert Dock warehouses — now being restored — while the rather more ramshackle structures in the foreground are on Manchester Dock, the former Liverpool base of the Mersey & Irwell Navigation Company. Between is the Pilotage building and the residences of Albert Pierhead, now part of the Merseyside Maritime Museum. *MCM*

from the technology which built the pyramids. It was possible to build steam-operated cranes, but these were of very limited value on a dock estate, where their boilers represented a serious fire hazard, their thermal efficiency was atrocious and they were a considerable maintenance liability. What was needed was a system which could distribute power from a central power station and which was safe, rugged and reliable. Liverpool, in common with other major ports, was reaching the point where ships and goods simply could not be handled fast enough to meet the available trade. Manpower was expensive, and horsepower took up too much space on already overcrowded quays. When William Armstrong built his first hydraulic crane, in Newcastle in 1846, it did not take long for Liverpool men to realise that there lay a possible answer to their problem of handling ever more goods. The following year the first four hydraulic machines from Armstrong's works were installed at the Albert Dock. Albert Dock warehouses were probably the first buildings in the world to be devised with mechanical cargo handling in mind — in advance of the machinery being available. From then on, virtually every dock which Hartley constructed or modernised was supplied with hydraulic power, employed not only for the operation of cranes and hoists, but also for capstans for warping ships around the docks, for movable bridges across the passages from one dock to another and for opening and closing the entrance and passage gates. In the case of cranes and hoists the benefit was calculated as a saving of some seven-eighths of the cost of manpower, while in the case of dock gate engines it may reasonably be assumed that another constraint on the maximum useful size of ship was removed.

Every new traffic gained by the Liverpool docks was likely to put more money into the hands of the minor ports around the estuary, as they played their part in the distribution of goods or raw materials. The growth of the cotton trade, for example, made Runcorn a much busier place, and the growth of the iron export trade greatly increased the traffic through Ellesmere Port, not only in iron goods downwards, but also in Furness haematite upwards. The traditional coal and salt traffics continued to grow: by the 1850s the tonnage of salt coming down the Weaver was over 600,000 per year and the growth in the demand for coal seemed to be endless. Nothing, it seemed, apart from the occasional (and dreaded) cyclical recession, could go wrong. The discovery of gold in Australia, for example, was not just a bonanza for the diggers, but also for those who could carry emigrants there, and all the multitude who could supply the goods the emigrants needed when they got there — tools, barbed wire, corrugated iron, etc. Because the Mersey was where the mercantile skills to get the ships and the goods together were to be found, it was through Ellesmere Port that much of the ironmongery passed, on its way to Liverpool, bound for Australia.

As in Liverpool, there was something of a lull in growth at the minor ports, during and shortly after the Napoleonic Wars, followed by some quite intensive building in the late 1820s and early 1830s, and this pattern repeats itself all round the estuary.

Runcorn may serve as a starting point: by 1828 the 'new line' of locks, which diverged from the old line three locks from the top and joined directly into the river immediately downstream of the old tidal basin, was completed. Between the old and new lines a number of minor improvements, and the construction of a substantial new basin, took place. Soon afterwards a new tidal basin was added, embracing the old basin entrance and the bottom lock of the new line of locks. The capacity of the locks was greatly increased both for canal and estuary craft, and the way pointed for continued expansion to the downstream side as time went on.

Just upstream, the rival Mersey & Irwell undertaking was also building, with a new entrance lock alongside the old and a very substantial basin completed by 1829. Downstream at Weston Point the Weaver Trustees enlarged their basin in 1833, installed a second entrance lock in 1837 and in 1839 made further enlargements on the south side of the basin.

On the Lancashire shore the Sankey proprietors must have been watching these steps to minimise the difficulties of getting boats in and out of docks: in 1830 they decided that the best way to avoid the problems of the channel up to Sankey Bridges was to follow the example of the Mersey & Irwell, by constructing a downstream extension to Widnes. They did not get there first, for earlier the same year the St Helens & Runcorn Gap Railway had been promoted, and in February 1833 the line was officially opened. Like the Liverpool & Manchester it had been 'sold' as a means of communication between the Mersey and its industrial hinterland: unlike its more prestigious rival it owned its access to the river, and at Widnes the company made history by completing the first purpose-built railway dock in the world. The canal company, whose enabling act had actually been passed on the same day as that for the railway, got its extension completed in July

the same year. There was no terminal basin, as in the other canal ports, but the section immediately above the entrance locks was of considerable width, allowing it to serve as a long narrow dock. The meeting of Widnes with its malodorous destiny as a chemicals town lay still in the future, but it had become quite an important transhipment centre for the thriving industries of St Helens.

Ellesmere Port had suffered somewhat from its origins in one of the grander schemes of the canal mania, but in 1826 Parliament gave its blessing to a scheme for a Birmingham & Liverpool Junction canal which would join the Ellesmere Canal with the Birmingham canals. Any canal which could link the burgeoning productive wealth of the 'Workshop of the World' with the thriving commerce of the Mersey could not fail, and in 1828 Thomas Telford was sent to re-plan Ellesmere Port to receive the anticipated upsurge in traffic. The scheme he produced involved a dock capable of accommodating sea-going ships, but which had arms extending under the wings of a great E-shaped warehouse, where barges could unload under cover. The first floor of this warehouse was at the level of the quay of an improved upper basin. An inner basin, on the same level as the dock, had numerous small arms protruding in the same sort of 'inkblot' shape used at Runcorn. The flight of locks remained unchanged, except that the two upper ones were paralleled by two new narrow ones. The scheme was not com-

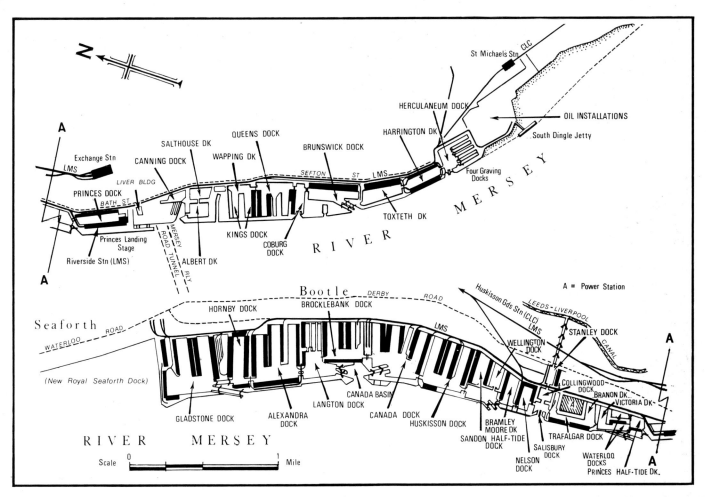

N
St Michaels Stn
CLC
HERCULANEUM DOCK
OIL INSTALLATIONS
South Dingle Jetty
HARRINGTON DK
Four Graving Docks
A
QUEENS DOCK
SALTHOUSE DK
BRUNSWICK DOCK
Exchange Stn
LMS
CANNING DOCK
WAPPING DK
SEFTON ST
LMS
LIVER BLDG
PRINCES DOCK
BATH ST
TOXTETH DK
MERSEY
KINGS DOCK
Princes Landing Stage
MERSEY RLY
ROAD TUNNEL
COBURG DOCK
RIVER
Riverside Stn (LMS)
ALBERT DK
A
Bootle
DERBY ROAD
A = Power Station
Huskisson Gds Stn (CLC)
LEEDS-LIVERPOOL CANAL
HORNBY DOCK
BROCKLEBANK DOCK
LMS
Seaforth
WATERLOO ROAD
WELLINGTON DOCK
STANLEY DOCK
LMS
A
(New Royal Seaforth Dock)
COLLINGWOOD DOCK
BRANON DK.
VICTORIA DK
CANADA BASIN
LANGTON DOCK
GLADSTONE DOCK
ALEXANDRA DOCK
CANADA DOCK
HUSKISSON DOCK
BRAMLEY MOORE DK
SANDON HALF-TIDE DOCK
TRAFALGAR DOCK
RIVER MERSEY
SALISBURY DOCK
WATERLOO DOCKS
Scale 0 1 Mile
NELSON DOCK
A
PRINCES HALF-TIDE DK.

pleted until 1843, but at one stride it placed Ellesmere Port in the front rank of transhipment ports. Only one significant improvement remained to be made, namely the installation of hydraulic power in 1876: apart from that, Telford's scheme was good enough to see out the life of Ellesmere Port's role as a transhipment port and carry it into its new life as a petrochemicals centre.

A success story as striking as that of early 19th century Liverpool would produce many winners, but it would also produce a few losers, including the Liverpool shipbuilding trade and the fishermen, progressively squeezed from the foreshore by the spread of new docks.

Meanwhile, the rapidly growing railway companies not only enjoyed bad relations with the Dock Committee but would, in any case, wish to avoid too much dependence upon any one such body. Two major railway companies did not have what they wanted in Liverpool: the Great Western Railway (GWR) had no foothold at all, and the London & North Western Railway (LNWR) did not have the direct access to docks it sought. These and other dissident elements were the stimuli to the development of docks on Wallasey Pool, a tidal inlet on the Wirral shore. Some important individuals had long nurtured such an idea: most notable perhaps was William Laird, but there were two Liverpool men who were hedging their bets, namely Sir John Tobin who was well known as a Liverpool Corporation member, and even more dubiously John Askew, the harbour master of the port. By 1830 all of these owned land on Wallasey Pool and no less a personage than Thomas Telford had been engaged to report on the possibilities for development. Sadly, when the time for action came it was not executed to the standard we might expect from such auspicious beginnings.

Above:
The docks of Liverpool. This map is of composite date to show the maximum extent of the system.

Below:
For the task of removing the 'muck' from the hole there were alternatives to the hideously dangerous barrow-runs which helped make navvying about the most dangerous job there was. Here the end-tippers are delivered by horse to a pair of steam travellers. These must have been very safe — observe the confidence of the man with the staff. *MCM*

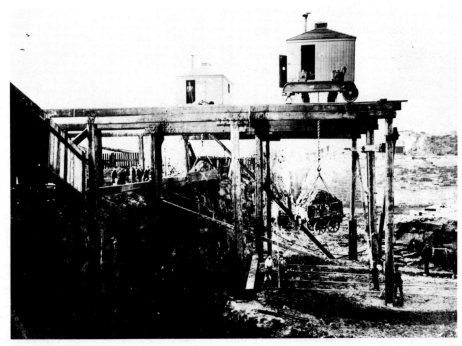

example of Thomas Brassey failing: the man who was to become Birkenhead's most prosperous son and the world's greatest railway contractor tried to retrieve the situation in 1854, but was unable to mobilise sufficient funds to overcome the difficulties. The badly-engineered and worse-financed 'competitor' lurched onwards towards disaster until 1858, when it succumbed to the inevitable in the form of incorporation in the new Mersey Docks & Harbour Board. Jesse Hartley was to succeed where others had failed and complete a useful dock system, no longer a competitor to Liverpool but a subsidiary.

The practice of moving downstream to get better access to deeper water had far from run its course. The coal traffic from

A good deal of intrigue went on the background, but the Birkenhead Dock Co was successfully formed and appointed J. M. Rendel as its engineer. In 1844 an enabling act was obtained and by 1847 Egerton and Morpeth Docks were open, but behind this apparently expeditious work lay engineering difficulties and overspending, which left the scheme incomplete with all the money gone. For two years nothing happened. Rendel had been criticised heavily for his mishandling of the scheme, and in July 1849 he resigned, but his replacement fared no better. So ill-starred, indeed, was the scheme that it even provides us with a rare

Below:
Map of Birkenhead Docks showing railway depots.

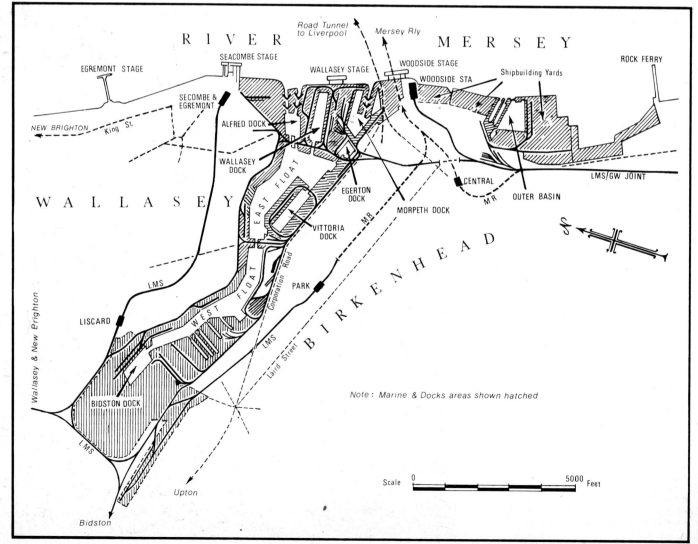

the St Helens coalfield, which had originally emerged into the Mersey at Warrington, had not moved far enough down when it came to Widnes, for the canal and the railway dock there were both inaccessible to anything bigger than a Mersey flat, and not constantly and easily available even to those. This was a particular disadvantage to the railway: apart from its having constructed the dock, it has another, less desirable, claim to fame, in that it was the only railway to have opened in competition with a canal, only to be soundly thrashed by the canal. As late as 1850 its coal traffic was only a small fraction of that on the canal. A major reason for this was that the boats which could conveniently load at Widnes could also get all the way up to St Helens — thereby eliminating the labour and breakage costs of transhipment from rail to boat. What the railway needed was access to deep water, where coal for export could be loaded directly into sea- or ocean-going vessels. The chosen site was at Garston, and in 1846 Parliamentary sanction was obtained for the building of an extension of the railway with a dock at the end of it. The work was completed and opened in 1853, being vastly superior to anything which might have been possible at Widnes. Not only was it capable of taking substantial ships but it was also able to bring coal trains in at a convenient height for tipping into hold (or bunker) with the minimum of manpower. The facilities were good enough to make Garston a potential competitor with Liverpool in some traffics, especially coal export, and this potential did not pass unobserved by one large and powerful organisation which did not like to be reliant on the Port of Liverpool.

In 1851 the LNWR had leased the assets of the Shropshire Union Railway & Canal Co, obtaining thereby a means of intruding into GWR territory in the Black Country area, and equally important, some very decent (if small-scale) shipping facilities at Ellesmere Port. The investment in Ellesmere Port which followed makes it quite clear that the policy was not at all the usual one of acquiring a canal and killing it by neglect: the LNWR really wanted Ellesmere Port as a way of partially escaping from Liverpool's stranglehold on the Mersey. In 1864 the company made a better move in the same direction when it swallowed the tiny St Helens & Runcorn Gap Railway, thereby obtaining the use of Garston Docks. Here again, it sought to

Right:

This is the reason for the silting of Wallasey Dock: the engines of Wallasey Impounding Station. Built by Gwynne's of Hammersmith in 1886 they pumped water from the river via three 54in intake pipes into the dock, which thus became, in effect, a sediment chamber for the rest of the system. They made good water losses, and were capable of providing an abnormally high level if necessary. In 1955 they were made redundant by a steam turbine plant built alongside; they lay derelict for many years before being broken for scrap. *AEJ*

make the best of the asset it had acquired, with substantial investment in improvements to the sidings and handling facilities. In 1867 an enabling act was obtained for the building of the North Dock, completed in 1876 and, like what was thenceforth called the Old Dock, well equipped with coal drops. Partly as cause and partly as effect, the industrial base of Garston began to broaden with a resulting increase in the amount and variety of trade through the docks. By 1870 there was a large iron works, a special steels works, copper works and a large sawmill, to name just a few of the more important. Direct rail connection to such works became the normal means of bringing goods in and out.

The reign of Jesse Hartley had been so long and so productive that it might be imagined that his retirement would lead to a slackening of the pace of construction. Many of the men who had dominated the scene when Hartley began his work were past their prime as well. In Liverpool, however, it was not usual for the second generation to squander on country houses the money their fathers had made. As Henry Booth, for example, was nearing retirement, his nephews, Charles and Alfred, were showing that there would continue to be demand for new docks for some time yet, and that Hartley's successor would have plenty to do. In 1866 they sent

their first vessel up the Amazon. They were among the first to realise the trading potential of a river which was readily navigable for over a thousand miles inland, and in 1874 they started trading at Manaus. From then until 1913 (when competition from rubber produced in plantations in Asia became serious) they participated in another of those great worldwide boom traffics for which 19th century Liverpudlians had such an infallible nose, the production and shipping of wild rubber.

No trade, no country was safe from Liverpool enterprise. The tea trade had long been a luxury traffic, dominated by London, and the passage to China had been the preserve of the most glamorous of the great sailing ships. On those routes the supreme elegance and efficiency of clippers with famous names like *Fiery Cross*, or *Cutty Sark* ruled. In 1865 the *Ariel* and the *Taeping* had raced to be the first home with the new growth. For 99 days skippers and crews had taxed their skill and endurance to the limit to extract every last fraction of a horsepower from the acres of sail under their control. Over those 99 days, the difference between them amounted to 12min: it was the supreme conflict of its kind, and the last to have any relevance.

Alfred Holt was another member of that Liverpool Unitarian community which included the Booths, and latterly the

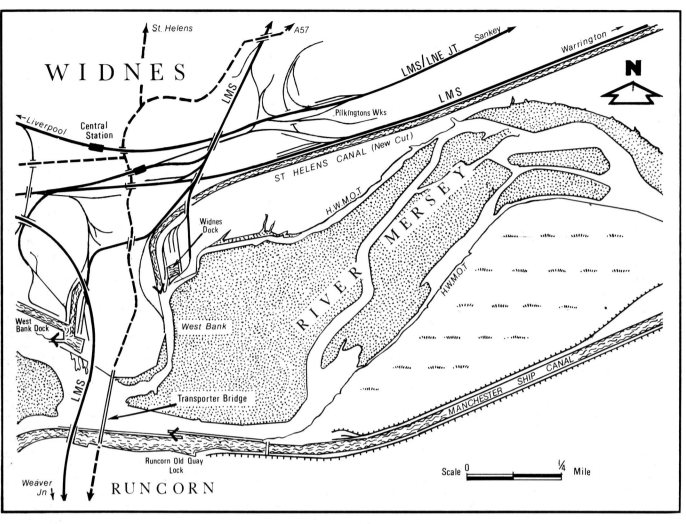

WIDNES

St. Helens
A57
Sankey
LMS/LNE JT.
Warrington
LMS
N
← Liverpool
Central Station
LMS
Pilkingtons Wks
ST HELENS CANAL (New Cut)
H.W.M.O.T
RIVER MERSEY
Widnes Dock
H.W.M.O.T
West Bank Dock
West Bank
LMS
MANCHESTER SHIP CANAL
Transporter Bridge
Scale 0 ¼ Mile
Runcorn Old Quay Lock
Weaver Jn
RUNCORN

Map of Widnes showing docks and railway connections.

Rathbones. He was the man who set himself the problem of reaching the Far East by steam. The reason for the continued success of the sailing ships on the really long passsage was that steam-ships required so much coal for such a distance that they were not only a poor financial proposition in terms of running costs, but also basically uneconomic in terms of the amount of space available for cargo after allowing for suitably huge bunkers. The solution lay in improving the thermal efficiency of the engines and in getting into a high value trade capable of 'carrying' the dead space of large bunkers. In 1865 Holt's Ocean Steam Ship Co received a new steamer from Scott's of Greenock. Called *Agamemnon*, she was moderately large at 309ft long and 2,279 gross tons, but what was important was that she had large bunkers and compound engines (using the exhaust from a small high pressure cylinder as the supply to a larger low pressure cylinder). In the following year she brought tea from China in 62 days. Ten years later, the Ocean Steam Ship Co owned 16 substantial steamships, all but one of them with compound engines, and the sailing ship was virtually dead on the Far East routes.

These were busy times for the Holt family, for while all this was going on,

Alfred's brother George was busy opening up another of Liverpool's growth markets. In 1865 the Liverpool, Brazil & River Plate Steam Navigation Co began trading, mainly in Brazilian coffee and Argentine meat. This proved to be the beginning of a very large trade, with substantial traffic in the export direction as well. A high proportion of the Argentine railway system passed through the Port of Liverpool, as

did the entire sewage disposal machinery of Buenos Aires.

The early 1860s had been a difficult time. The cotton trade was by now very heavily dependent on the North American raw material, cotton from other sources being almost negligible. The American Civil War looked from the start as though it would seriously damage the market. The naval blockade imposed by the North caused

Liverpool men problems in getting the cotton through, but also offered the prospect of making large amounts of money in other ways. They flouted the Government's policy of neutrality and indeed some openly advocated declaring war on the North. They sold arms, including the devastatingly successful commerce raider *Alabama*, to the south: on occasions they even organised collections for little tokens of their appreciation to be sent to the South, like the Whitworth Gun which arrived at Fort Fisher. Their most significant activity, however, was blockade-running. This was not actually illegal but it was extremely dangerous, and could come close to piracy. The South, however, had plenty of money and a serious shortage of war supplies, a combination irresistible to any red-blooded Liverpudlian. The result was the development of an entirely new kind of ship: small, shallow, built entirely of steel rather than iron, and breathtakingly fast. The profits were as impressive as the speed: despite the fact that the skipper and crew could earn as much on one trip through the blockade as they might in an average year's peacetime sailing, these ships typically paid off their entire capital cost on the first trip. On one celebrated occasion the Liverpool yard of Jones, Quiggin launched five of them on the same day. Whereas large areas of south Lancashire were reduced quite literally to famine conditions, with charitable collections being held for famine relief as far afield as Washington and St Petersburg, Liverpool not only survived through its flexibility but raised substantial funds for the relief of cotton workers as well. When the war was over not only were there some very rich people around with money to invest, but also a great deal had been learned about the new skills of steel shipbuilding.

In the midst of this expansion of Liverpool trade all over the world, one area stood out as having witnessed a marked decline. In West Africa the main traffic had been, until 1807 (when the last slave ship sailed), in West Africans. From then until about 1850 there had been a definite growth in trade, especially in palm

oil to supply the growing soap industry and the beginnings of margarine manufacture, but in a number of other commodities as well. It was hampered by a number of difficulties, not least the high fatality rate among Europeans attempting to live and trade in the 'White Man's Grave' and the lack of a scheduled steamship service. In 1852, William Macgregor Laird (of the Birkenhead shipbuilding family) eventually succeeded in supplying the shipping deficiency by the establishment of the African Steamship Co. This was at first London-based, but moved to Liverpool in 1856, where better mercantile skills soon made it a successful undertaking. On its staff was a man who was destined to become one of the most powerful of Liverpool's shipping magnates, Alfred Lewis Jones. In 1878 he set up on his own account as Alfred L. Jones & Co and the following year he also joined Elder Dempster & Co. By 1884 he had gained control of the latter firm, and through it control of a great proportion of the shipping of West African goods. Because of the deficiency of harbours on the West African coast, goods were generally lightered to and from ships in surf boats, and Jones next gained control of these, which meant that rival vessels sometimes faced mysterious delays in loading or discharging cargoes. Numerous attempts were made to break his stranglehold, which had been further tightened by the establishment of the West African Shipping Conference in 1895, all of them unsuccessful.

The practical result of this virtual monopoly of trade with an important area for the production of primary commodities was not only that the value of trade from British West Africa rose from £252,814 in 1852 to £1,099,256 by 1884, but also that a much larger proportion of it came to Liverpool. Particularly significant was the increase in palm oil from £101,631 to £592,448, and perhaps, even more so the rise in kernels for oil from a mere £844 to £284,707. The latter was the basis of one of

Merseyside's growth industries, seed oil pressing, which remains important to this day. Of course, traditional trades like timber importing also flourished and there was, until the collapse of the wild rubber trade, a considerable and growing traffic in rubber too.

—————

Back on the Dock Estate, the growth of traffic from all over the world was having the obvious consequences. Money was very readily available for investment in new dock facilities and the demand for their use was seemingly insatiable. Not only were there more and more companies requiring more and more appropriated berths for their new traffics, but there was a need for modernisation of existing docks. During the second half of the century the average size of ship using the docks rose from about 3,000 tons to about 10,000 tons, with the obvious result that old entrances and quays became inadequate. New docks were added to the system: at the north end, Canada Half-tide (later converted and renamed Brocklebank Dock) was opened in 1862, followed by Langton and Alexandra in 1881. In 1884 the last new dock to be added at the north for over 40 years was opened and named Hornby Dock. Additions at the south end continued. In 1864 Herculaneum Dock was opened, providing what was probably the first purpose-built petroleum storage, a number of rock 'casemates' excavated into a cliff face and provided with sturdy iron doors, while the southern system was 'completed' with the addition of Harrington in 1883 and Toxteth in 1888.

Just as important as the new construction was a massive programme of modernisation which took place on the South Docks over much of the second half of the century. The system had grown up piecemeal, and had not really become a system at all. Lyster's task was to convert what was there to a spine and branch

system, making as much quay space as possible available to the largest possible ships. This involved the abolition of some old river entrances, the reconstruction of others, widespread alterations of passages between docks, and in many cases extensive alterations to the shapes of the docks themselves. Some, such as Queen's Dock, emerged from this process almost unrecognisable; while Salthouse Dock was moved bodily through being reduced on one side and enlarged on the other.

The increase which was sought was, it must be remembered, an increase in the throughput of goods, so that the problem did not begin and end with the mere provision of quay space or depth of water. It was also necessary to increase the rate at which goods could be loaded and unloaded. The hydraulic system which had begun at Albert was extended to cover the whole of the South Docks, with substantial new pumping stations at Brunswick and Herculaneum. To provide shelter and working space for the increased flow of goods, new and larger transit sheds, many of them with completely clear span roofs, were constructed on a large proportion of the quaysides. Some of these were two-storey structures enabling goods to be unloaded yet more rapidly, and many of them were constructed on the new 'Hennebique' system of concrete construction. The bottleneck thus moved to the carters and waggoners who removed the goods from the transit sheds, and a belated realisation of the facts of life led to a greatly enhanced provision of railway facilities — though it was not to be until 1904 that the Dock Board would take the final step of acquiring and operating its own fleet of shunting locomotives. The improved loading and unloading equipment was supplemented by great improvements in the movable bridges on the passages, nearly all of which were replaced or converted for operation by hydraulic power, as were most of the entrance and passage gates. This resulted in easier movements of ships in and out of the berths, and further improvements were brought about by the provision of steam impounding pumps which made it much easier to maintain adequate water levels in the docks during sequences of low tides. Similar modernisation was proceeding in the older parts of the North Docks, and on the Birkenhead side. Lyster's work is not of such a flamboyant character as Hartley's, and he did not construct as many new docks, but his achievements in keeping pace with the growth of trade brought about by the energy and acumen of

Liverpool shipowners and merchants must not be underestimated. They took some keeping up with.

Liverpool still had new traffics to come. On the Birkenhead side there had long been an extensive traffic in live animals to the abattoirs, the Mersey being a major market for imported meat. New developments were afoot towards the end of the century which called forth another of Liverpool's great enterprises. The preservation of food by canning had been employed in a somewhat unscientific way during the Napoleonic Wars, but steady progress in both the theory and the practice of canning had eventually led to a huge meat-canning industry in Chicago in the late 1860s. Samuel Vestey was a Liverpool provision merchant who had been successful on a modest scale, and when his son William was old enough to take up employment in the family firm it was, among other places in the United States, to Chicago that he went, primarily to buy goods. There William learned that the problem with food supply was not production — the productive capacity of the New World was seemingly infinite — but of finding ways of preserving food for transport. On his return to Britain he set up in partnership with his younger brother Edmund in 1885, when the brothers were aged respectively 26 and 19. Their mercantile activities made them some considerable profit, and in 1897 they established the Union Cold Storage & Ice Co Ltd. The first meat-freezing works in the world had been built (in Australia) as long ago as 1861 and the first ocean voyage by a refrigerated vessel loaded with meat had been in 1877. The largest potential supplier was, the Vesteys thought, Argentina, a

country William had visited some years previously. The timing of their venture was impeccable: in 1880 Argentina produced 3,571 frozen carcasses and in 1900 this had risen to 2,332,837. Of course, entrepreneurs in the Vestey class did not depend on a single traffic: they also imported frozen meats from Australia and New Zealand and fruit from South America. Whilst trying a not very successful venture in frozen pork from China they not only discovered that frozen chickens were a better idea, but also pioneered the importing of chilled eggs. By 1910 a few problems with shipowners coupled with an availability of capital led to the purchase of their first ship, the refrigerated *Indraghiri*. Two further ships followed the next year and thus was born the Blue Star Line.

It was, of course, necessary to provide cold storage at Liverpool for the reception of imports. Part of the virtually obsolete Albert Dock warehouses was converted, as was Liverpool's first theatre, the Theatre Royal, but these were insignificant compared with the purpose-built giant at Alexandra or its successor at Canada. Among Liverpool's less known superlatives was that it could for many years boast the largest egg-breaking plant in the world, another offshoot of the Vestey empire. William Vestey was created a Baronet in 1913, followed in 1922 by his brother Edmund. In 1922 Sir William, perhaps the last of Liverpool's truly great trading pioneers, became Baron Vestey of Kingswood.

In Birkenhead the inauspicious start had been left behind. The remaining schemes of Rendel were completed by 1863, with the opening of the Low-Water Basin, which was later converted into Wallasey

Dock. The total acreage was now very nearly 140, and no further major construction occurred until this century. Hydraulic power arrived for the operation of the gates, movable bridges, etc, in the impressive shape of the Central Hydraulic Tower in 1863, and in 1886 another large piece of plant was purchased when the Wallasey Dock Impounding Station was built to maintain levels within the system by means of some very large steam pumps. 1879 saw another growth area when new facilities for landing live cattle from North America and Argentina were opened, making Birkenhead a major centre not only of meat supply but in leather production and in all the animal by-product trades.

Trade further up the river was still growing, and both the Runcorn and Weston Point Docks saw further expansion. In 1860 the Alfred Dock was completed by the Bridgewater Trustees, connecting via the new Runcorn & Weston Canal with the Weaver Docks at Weston Point. The narrow Francis Dock (opened before 1850) connected with the new line of locks and the building of Arnold and Fenton Docks (in 1870 and 1875 respectively) completed the circuit, linking all the docks one to another and giving all the connection with Weston Point. At the other end of that short (and rather

Below:
Entry into the docks of the lower part of the estuary has never been particularly easy. A bulk carrier is seen entering at Alfred Basin (with the ubiquitous Hartley copings in the foreground) with the aid of two tugs. Although it is near slack water, the unladen condition of the ship is making the after tug work for its living, as the pall of black smoke testifies. *AEJ*

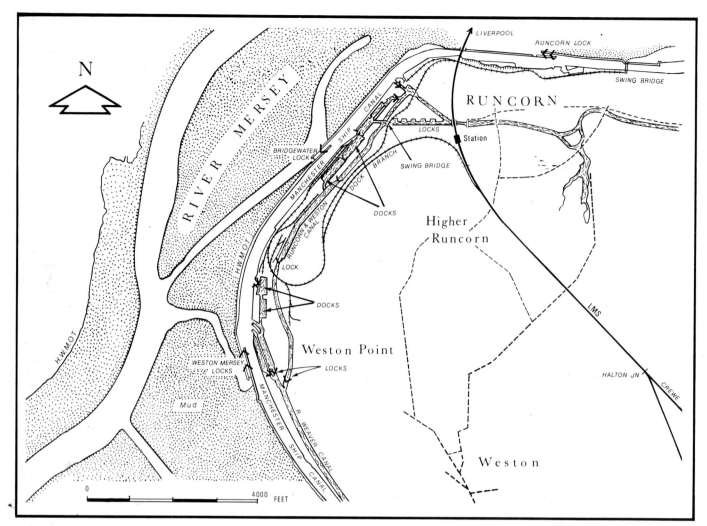

Map labels: N, RIVER MERSEY, LIVERPOOL, RUNCORN LOCK, SWING BRIDGE, RUNCORN, LOCKS, Station, BRIDGEWATER LOCK, MANCHESTER SHIP CANAL, RUNCORN & WESTON CANAL, DOCK BRANCH, DOCKS, SWING BRIDGE, Higher Runcorn, LOCK, H.W.M.O.T., DOCKS, WESTON MERSEY LOCKS, Weston Point, LOCKS, LMS, HALTON JN, CREWE, Mud, MANCHESTER SHIP CANAL, R. WEAVER CANAL, Weston, 0, 4000 FEET, H.W.M.O.T.

Above:

Map of Runcorn: composite date to show maximum extent of the docks at Old Quay, Runcorn Docks and Weston Point.

unsuccessful) canal, the Weaver Trustees had catered for the growing chemicals trade by improving the river walls and entrances and adding Delamere Dock (opened by 1870); Tollemache Dock followed in 1885. The following year sealed the question of further expansion, when a competitor far more formidable than any railway first appeared. Ships could compete with trains, and the Weaver had now been so enlarged that coasters could get up to Northwich, but neither could compete with brine pipelines.

Widnes had, from an early date, held an unsavoury reputation as a place where chemical manufacturers could get away with almost any form of pollution they could perpetrate, and one cannot deny that they were inventive in discovering new and ever fouler ways of assailing the earth, air and water of Widnes. Huge growth in chemical output occurred, but this was not reflected in anything very impressive in the way of dock building; in fact only the little West Bank Dock, a long narrow basin for flats, with two arms, was constructed: the channel to Widnes was not good and the greater part of its expansion was based on rail transport.

In the same way that Liverpool had needed to accommodate ever-growing ships, so there was also a demand for larger vessels to be accepted in the small ports of the upper Mersey. Garston and Ellesmere Port were served by good, deep natural

channels close in to the shore, but finding the way into Runcorn or Weston Point was definitely not for beginners. The channels were not very good and they shifted frequently, problems with which the Mersey flatmen, born and bred there, could cope (usually), but which were much more formidable to the German skipper of a 300-ton schooner bound for Runcorn. In 1876 the Upper Mersey Navigation Commission was established, composed of representatives of bodies having an interest in the use of the upper estuary with powers to buoy and light the channels above Eastham and as far as Bank Quay, Warrington. From their surviving charts, updated each year, it is clear that the Commission's buoy tender/survey vessel/maid-of-all-work the *Jesse Wallwork* had plenty to do in following the vagaries of the ever-mobile sandbanks. Looking at the upper Mersey at low tide today, it is difficult to understand how it could have been navigated before the work of the Commission.

There had long been dreams of more radical improvements above Eastham, with particular reference to the drastic up-grading of the route of the old Mersey & Irwell Navigation. The initiative was from Manchester, where considerable disillusionment with the status quo existed. This probably began with the Liverpool & Manchester Railway, which had been launched with pious statements about the

benefits of competition. Within a year of its opening it had already entered into a rate-fixing agreement with the canal companies, and it went on to become the most expensive railway in the country in terms of rates per ton per mile.

Because the Liverpool Docks had begun as a municipal undertaking, ships using them were liable to two charges — Dock Dues and Town Dues, the latter being waived to Liverpool Freemen. In 1858 Town Dues had been abolished in consideration of the receipt by the newly formed Mersey Docks & Harbour Board of a lump-sum commutation payment. Town Dues, however, eventually reappeared, to the fury of consignees in and around Manchester. Even apart from this issue, Liverpool was not only an expensive port to use, but a somewhat complicated one from the point of view of paperwork. Dock Dues, porterage rates, warehousing rates and cartage rates were all fixed, with immense lists of different rates for different classes of items. The problem was that these lists were not the same. To take a trifling example, there was a specific rate of Dock Dues for capsicums, but for all other charges they had to be fitted into some other category — they only appear in one

of the four lists. Mancunians began to see Liverpool as an unscrupulously operated toll bar on a natural waterway to which they considered they had as much right as did the Liverpudlians. In this view they were not without some justification, though they seem to have given less than the credit which was due for the buoying, lighting, dredging and training walls paid for by Liverpool which alone made possible access to the Mersey for ships of the size in which their goods came. Neither were they willing to admit what they surely knew, that the charge for port services was and always had been determined by what the traffic would bear.

If the Bill for the Liverpool & Manchester Railway was a long hard struggle for the merchants and shipowners of Liverpool, the campaign for its passage was easy going indeed compared with the problems faced by the Manchester men when they sought an act for the building of a ship canal. This was a bold, if not heroic, bid to take ships straight to Manchester, eliminating transhipment to barge or railway in Liverpool; of course it attracted ferocious opposition in Liverpool, as it did also from a number of interests in the minor ports, and even from individuals. Speke Hall, a couple of miles above Garston, had stood for several centuries without having ships at the bottom of its garden, and Miss Adelaide Watt saw no reason why she should have them now: the proposed canal was moved to the Cheshire shore to eliminate her opposition. Three times the Bill went to Parliament. In 1883 the Commons Committee passed it and the Lords threw it out; in 1884 the Lords passed it and the Commons did not and in 1885 it was passed. The real struggle had been in 1884, when 151 witnesses spent 38 days answering 25,367 questions. One of them said too much: Lyster, when giving evidence of the harm which would result to the estuary from the scheme proposed, was drawn into saying how such harm could be avoided, and his suggestions were gratefully accepted and incorporated into the plan for the final successful application.

The building and financing of Britain's last great inland waterway was almost as problematical as the obtaining of the act. Surrounded by the scornful utterances of the railway propaganda departments, which missed no opportunity to decry canals as obsolete and incapable of useful service in the modern world, the Mancunians soldiered doggedly on, and on 1 January 1894 their great canal was opened, semi-officially, by a procession of craft led by the steam yacht *Norseman*. On 21 May the official ceremony took place when Queen Victoria, aboard the *Enchantress*, sailed part of its length. The long campaign had at last turned Manchester into a seaport.

The installations of the Ship Canal are in a sense part of the story of the Mersey, and in another are deliberately no part at all of that story. The purpose of the canal was, after all, to avoid using the facilities of the lower Mersey. The implementation of this purpose, however, had very definite implications in the Upper Mersey, whether the promoters liked it or not, as their canal cut off from the river all the minor ports on the Cheshire shore — Ellesmere Port, Weston Point, Runcorn and Frodsham. The Old Quay terminus ceased to exist, becoming a depot for the Ship Canal's craft and maintenance facilities, and much of the bed of the old Navigation disappeared under the new canal. The Bridgewater was bought, and Runcorn Docks became part of the Port of Manchester. The interests of those who depended on access to these ports for small craft were protected in the enabling act, and despite the widespread opposition in the small ports to the building of the Ship Canal, it actually brought substantial benefits to them by enabling much larger ships to reach them. In each case it was possible for ships too large for the old docks to tie up in the Ship Canal, against what had been the river wall. This was to arrest decline in both Runcorn and Weston Point and bring a new prosperity to Ellesmere Port. In 1899 a large new granary was built there, followed by a small new dock (known as the Mill Arm) behind it, and three large steam flour mills. The first decade of this century saw the access to ocean shipping attract the Wolverhampton Corrugated Iron Co to Ellesmere Port, which was so large an undertaking that it alone changed the base of the local economy from transport and distribution to manufacturing.

Dire effects had been foreseen in Liverpool. The prophets of doom had been wrong again about the dire effects on the channels in the estuary, and they were, at least to begin with, wrong about the commercial effects on Liverpool as well. The Ship Canal was successful, but only modestly so, for Liverpool's commercial muscle was sufficient to prevent many potential users going to Manchester. It might also be argued that there was, at least until the opening years of this century, sufficient additional swill going into the trough to allow another pig to get its snout in. The years from 1907-14 were not, however, an Edwardian Indian Summer for Liverpool: they were the years when the growth rate really began to

slacken, and when the proportion of ships which only paid harbour dues (ie, those which entered the Mersey but berthed elsewhere) began to rise sharply, reaching 21% in 1913. It was not a catastrophic loss, but it was a very noticeable one, and it must be largely attributable to the Ship Canal.

By the outbreak of World War 1 we have seen the construction of nearly all the docks on the Mersey, and we have seen established the patterns which will be visible as the great second port of Empire, owning about 14% of all the shipping in the world, begins to metamorphose into what it is today.

Above:
Despite the fact that the Ship Canal was originally intended to turn Manchester into a seaport, the docks built at Stanlow have for some considerable time been more important. The tanks, farms and refineries to which the berths are connected extend over thousands of acres. In this postwar view, evidence of wartime camouflage paint schemes applied to dockside buildings can be seen in the upper portion of the picture. *IAL*

Below:
In this more recent view the industry which depends on the docks has sprawled across the Stanlow Meadows, Ince Hall and Manor, engulfed the village of Ince and started on its way on to Ince Marshes. *PoM*

Entr'acte:
The Mersey Docks
& Harbour Board in 1937

There are various years one might choose to illustrate the zenith of the Mersey Docks & Harbour Board's wealth and power, most of them significant in one way or another. 1937 has here been chosen because it was the year in which, for the port's purposes, the depression of the 1930s might be said to have ended. Since the end of World War 1, there had been some very bad years, although it must be remembered that all but the very worst of them still represented a higher level of traffic than that of the supposed Edwardian swansong. 1936 had seen an encouraging year, with traffic up to 21.02 million tons; 1937 fulfilled the Board's hopes with 21.39 million. Whilst with the benefit of hindsight we can see severe relative decline, in simple tonnage terms there was nothing wrong.

The Dock Estate as we know it today was all built apart from Royal Seaforth, and had a water area of nearly 182 acres on the Birkenhead side, with nearly 477 acres on the Liverpool side. The total length of quayside available to shipping on the Board's estate was over 38 miles. The largest entrance was that at Gladstone, 1,070ft long by 130ft wide — capable at a squeeze of taking either of the 'Queens' — but there were three other entrances of 600ft or more length, which was quite sufficient for any normally large merchant ship, and it must be remembered that the staple traffics of the port at that date were mostly carried in ships of under 10,000 tons.

Repair facilities in the graving docks were on an equally grand scale. A total of 17 graving docks had a total length of nearly 13,000ft, of which by far the largest was, once again, at Gladstone — 1,050ft long by 120ft wide. This monster among graving docks had been built with the intention of serving the largest transatlantic liners, although with the secondary intention of accommodating the super-dreadnoughts which were just appearing when it was opened in 1913. Seven of the lesser docks were over 600ft long.

These are, however, rather simple and obvious ways of showing the size of the Dock Board's undertaking, and they neglect a very large part of it. There was, for example, the small matter of a dock

Above:
The huge size of the passenger liners required enormous maintenance facilities. Gladstone Graving Dock, Liverpool, was built to be capable of taking the largest ships in the world at the time (1911), and whilst the first impression from this photograph is of the speed, grace and power of the vessel, it also gives a fair idea of the size. *MCM*

railway system of nearly 121 miles total length. In 1937 it handled a total of 206,993 loaded wagons behind its own locomotives, carrying 1.2 million tons of goods. It will be readily understood that this side of the business of the port, often regarded as peripheral, employed some 20 locomotives and a couple of hundred men. The amount of traffic it handled would, of course, have been more than many a small pre-Grouping railway company could hope for.

In addition to transport along the ground, the Board also provided large quantities of lifting appliances for transport in the vertical plane. In 1937 these were still mostly of relatively small capacity, for breakbulk cargoes, and the majority of them were driven by hydraulic power supplied from the Board's own pumping stations. There was a standby line to the Liverpool Hydraulic Power Co, but its pumping capacity was nowhere near that of the Board's. There were 191 hydraulic cranes between one and 40 tons, with most of the larger ones being associated with the coaling berths, though there was a 30-tonner at Langton Graving Dock. If the future of crane-driving lay with electricity, there

was a respectable advance guard of electric cranes in service, 122 in number, ranging from 13cwt to 15 tons. In addition to the old 87-ton steam crane shown in the photographs, which was the most powerful fixed crane on the estate, there were three lesser steam cranes. For the keep-fit enthusiasts there were still 18 hand cranes of from two to nine tons capacity. These 335 machines, every one of which required to be maintained and documented, were not the end of the story, for there were also the portable cranes — seven steam driven and two electric. Above all, in terms of versatility and cost, were the floating cranes: no less than five of these were in commission, all of them steamers. *Titan* was the baby of the family at a mere 25 tons, followed by *Samson* (30 tons), *Her-*

Above:

The size of Gladstone Entrance is well illustrated by the substantial container vessel *Mostangen* 'sharing' a lock with a smaller vessel already in position. In the background is ACL's *Atlantic Causeway*. *MD&HC*

cules (50 tons), *Atlas* (100 tons) and finally the aptly named *Mammoth* with a capacity of 200 tons.

Specialised handling and storage facilities were usually provided by the users, as in the case of the very large installations operated by the Liverpool Grain Storage & Transit Co Ltd, but some were provided by the Board. The livestock trade was provided with direct landing facilities serving Birkenhead Lairage and far beyond which had a ground area of over 98,000sq yd and could handle over 6,000 cattle and 12,000 sheep at one time. Bonded storage for 180,000 casks of tobacco existed at Stanley Dock, and the nearby wool warehouse could store 90,000 bales, 50,000 tons of grain, 60,000 barrels of oil, 38,000 tons of bulk oil — the list seems capable of almost infinite extension, and so it very nearly would be if all the general warehouses and the privately operated storage facilities were included.

The passenger traffic of Liverpool was no longer what it had been, but it was still sufficient to require the provision and maintenance of floating stages at Liverpool and Birkenhead (together with a third one at Wallasey for the cattle trade). The

Below:

By contrast, Gladstone Dock — last of the 'conventional' docks — was very open and spacious, as the roughness of the water on a windy day makes clear. The 10,000-ton *Patroclus* of the China Mutual Steam Navigation Co looks almost lost in the expanse of water. The three-storey concrete transit sheds used here and at Hornby increased the rate at which goods could be handled, but must be among the port's ugliest buildings. *MCM*

Birkenhead stage was used virtually exclusively by the ferries, which at that date still included the 'luggage boats' or goods ferries. The Liverpool Stage was a different matter. Home to many of the great liners, as well as to the short sea ferries, it was the longest floating structure in the world, 2,534ft long. It was provided with a sheltered 'upper deck' for much of its length, and also with direct access to the mainline railway system via the Board's riverside station alongside (whence trains could proceed to Edge Hill).

Little has been said about the problems of getting all these ships and goods into or out of the river. For the 10 previous years, the Board had removed an average of 17.6 million tons of sand and silt per year from various points in the river and estuary where it got in the way. The less glamorous items of the Engineer's Department fleet included the 19 self-propelled hopper barges which helped remove it. Mainly for use within the dock system were six self-propelled grab hopper dredgers, and next up in the order of seniority were the three bucket-ladder dredgers. For serious work in the approach channels the big sand pump dredgers were used: they were five in number, from the 3,500-ton *Hoyle* to the 10,000-ton *Leviathan*, the latter for many years the largest dredger in the world.

Of course the Engineer's Department was not the only one with a fleet of its own, although it was the largest. The Warehouse Department had seven grain barges, while the Marine Department had two tenders, five lightships, one salvage vessel, six survey launches, five 'camels' and five dummy barges. (Both the latter were used for salvage work.) The Pilotage Department weighed in with four pilot 'boats', which were in reality small ships capable of keeping station at sea, and a river launch. Of course the subject of navigation into the port also calls to mind the fact that the Board owned and maintained four lighthouses stretching as far away as Anglesey and a telegraph station on Hilbre Island.

The Board was an enormous organisation, with a turnover of millions of pounds a year. It controlled an estate of over 2,000 acres, excluding land bought for possible future development at Dingle, Seaforth and Tranmere and at its outstations. Figures are tedious, but it is perhaps only by 'zooming in' on the figures for just one year that we can comprehend the magnitude of the undertaking. It was scarcely surprising that, when war broke out, it should become the keypoint of the Battle of the Atlantic. It is sometimes forgotten that the war could have been as easily lost in the chilly waters of the Atlantic as in the air over the Home Counties.

Decline and Revival

World War 1 is generally recognised as having changed almost everything. It was possibly the first war in which there was ultimately no possible benefit for either side, so great was the destruction of life and property. Liverpool shipping was hard hit: of the 3 million tons of British merchant shipping sunk, mainly during the unrestricted U-boat campaign, over half had belonged to Liverpool companies, and at the same time foreign merchant tonnage had increased by some 7 million tons. This reduced substantially the overall competitive strength of British shipping, with a disproportionate loss borne by Liverpool. During the war the operation of the port was seriously disrupted by the loss of men to the Army, and in a distressingly high number of cases that loss was permanent. As happened with a number of other cities, one of the 'Pals' battalions — which had been recruited from specific neighbourhoods — was almost totally wiped out. The fate of 17th Battalion, The King's (Liverpool) Regiment was a disaster to south Liverpool whose social effects lasted for decades, and those effects spread through local shipping and industry as the loss of skilled and experienced workers.

There has long been a tendency to assume that almost everything reached its zenith in Edwardian England, that World War 1 upset the established way in which everything worked and decline has been more or less uniform ever since. This is possibly true in some instances, but certainly not true of the Port of Liverpool. Despite the enormous expansion in trade and in the physical facilities of the port, relative decline had already been setting in for some years. The growth rate was slackening and rivals getting stronger. It is important to remember that the decline of Liverpool remained relative only, for a long time: in 1898, 15,879 ships entered Liverpool and Birkenhead Docks while after 40 years of 'decline' this number had fallen to 12,334 and by 1984 to a mere 3,149. The catch is, of course, in the size of the ships, for the 1898 figure represents 7,800,000 registered tonnage of shipping, while that for 1938 was 16,500,000 tons. The 1984 figure conceals an actual goods tonnage of over 10 million, representing an enormous increase over a year in the supposed Indian summer of the port. Much of the talk of decline in Liverpool is more based on careful study of the popular press than on any attempt at understanding what has been going on.

The main reason that the port managed to continue to increase the tonnage using the docks between the wars was a bold attempt to keep abreast of developments and to do as previous generations had done by anticipating change. On the Birkenhead side, Bidston Dock was opened in 1933, but the most important development was the Gladstone complex at the northern extremity of the Liverpool Estate. The graving dock there had been planned and opened before the war to accommodate the largest ships afloat or reasonably foreseeable. There were those at the time who considered this to be an unwarrantable chasing after the 'glamour' trades, especially the great passenger liners. These, it was said, only provided the port's jam: its bread and butter came from freight liners of around 10,000 tons. When White Star and later Cunard moved to Southampton with their express services (though their 'slow boats' continued to use the Mersey) the critics seemed to have been proved right. Once more, with the benefit

Below:
Before World War 1 large amounts of cargo were moved about the estuary by the flats. This tiny dock, alongside the Pier Head, was Chester Basin, belonging to the Shropshire Union Railway and Canal Company. The press of boats in it speaks for itself. *MCM*

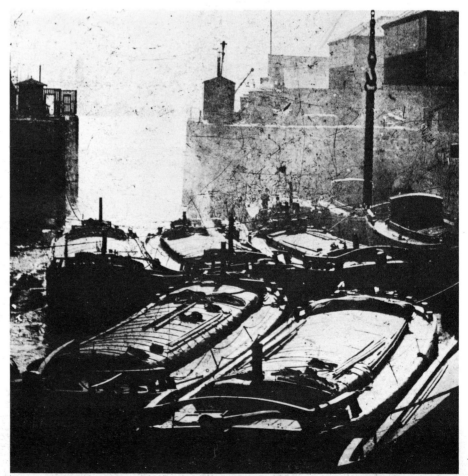

Right:
There's nothing new about traffic jams: the centre of attraction for the vehicles and the people is the last and largest of the Cunard 'four stackers'. *Aquitania* entered service in 1914 and represented a 50% tonnage increase over *Mauretania (I)*. *MCM*

of hindsight we can see that they were dangerously wrong, and be thankful that their arguments did not prevail. There could be no doubt that the trend of more goods in fewer larger ships was going to continue, and there was no shortage in Liverpool or elsewhere of berths for vessels of moderate size. Liverpool had always been an expensive port, and the reason that it could prosper whilst being undercut was that it offered better facilities and services. The complex was completed in 1927. It consisted of a large new entrance, the main dock, two branches and the graving dock — a total of 58¼ acres of water. It was directly rail-connected and adjacent to the very large North Mersey goods yard of the London Midland & Scottish (LMS) Railway. Its construction was a gamble on, and for, the future, and it was one which was to pay off. It kept Liverpool prosperous into the 1950s.

In addition to the new construction, the interwar years also saw some substantial modernisation programmes. The new three-storey concrete transit sheds at Gladstone were matched by new sheds on many other docks, and electric lifting appliances began to take over from hydraulic. The dock railway continued to be extended and to carry increasing

amounts of traffic. At the other extremity, Herculaneum Dock was gradually provided with equipment for oil handling and storage at the expense of its original role as a coaling berth, and the oil facilities spread southwards over land which had been acquired for possible expansion until an important oil jetty and tank farm were in existence stretching for a mile towards Garston. Other specialised facilities appeared, like the great granaries at Brunswick and Alexandra, dwarfing the

rather prettier ones built by Lyster at Waterloo and elsewhere. There was also a certain amount of modernisation of minor docks in order to free berths in larger ones, even such an unlikely place as the truncated remains of George's Dock Passage receiving a new transit shed, a

Below:
The Cunard White Star liner *Mauretania (II)* was launched on 28 July 1938 from Cammell Laird's yard at Birkenhead. *IAL*

Above:
At the extreme south of the docks was the connection to the Cheshire Lines, and yet further coaling berths at Herculaneum Dock. This branch dock would become an oil berth, but here in about 1900 we find two great hydraulic straddle cranes and topsail schooners still in evidence. In the background, the bridge carrying the Overhead Railway into Dingle Tunnel is visible. *MCM*

concrete quay surface and large modern bollards.

Garston had continued to expand: encouraged by the success of the docks, new industries had arrived, notably Wilson's Bobbin Works, the largest manufacturer of bobbins for the textile industry and the producer of some 5,000 gross of bobbins per year. The Garston Tanning Co started in 1900, processing 200 hides that year: by 1911 that figure had risen to 2,000. In short, everything was still rosy at Garston, and the opening of the new Stalbridge Dock in 1909 confirmed the spirit of optimism. Once the postwar recession was over, Garston continued to grow: by 1937 over one million tons of coal were exported each year, and a similar volume of imports was arriving. Like Liverpool, Garston had an eye for a new traffic and was early in the business of importing bananas. In 1912 it captured the Elders & Fyffes traffic from Manchester, landing 48,876 tons that year, but in 1929 it went in for high technology with four purpose-built banana elevators which could unload 120,000 bunches of bananas in a day. The docks were well equipped with hydraulic cranes and hoists, and could admit ships of up to 10,000 tons.

With hindsight we must suspect that Garston's days were numbered, for it was heavily dependent on coal and railways. Its 92 miles of sidings would not be much of an asset as the motor lorry began to take over, nor would its coal resist the influx of cheap oil. Events are not always predictable, however, and Garston was to receive a new lease of life.

There is one small port on the estuary which has so far escaped our attention altogether, and that is the little complex consisting of Bromborough Dock and Port Sunlight Dock. Both arose from the characteristic policy of William Lever of avoiding having his supplies under outside control. In 1895, after buying his way into West African Shipping, he constructed a small dock on Bromborough Pool for the offloading of oil seeds and similar products for his mills. The dock was rail-connected to what was to become probably the largest works railway system in the country, with some 52 miles of track, and thus to the booming Lever empire of soap and oleochemicals.

When the Storeton Tramway made its noisy way down to Bromborough Pool in 1838 there was already a quay there, used for the transport of stone, and this remained in use until 1906. In 1923 the new Bromborough Dock gained an enabling act and in 1926 the first ship was loaded there, although the official opening did not take place until 1931. It was an altogether larger undertaking than the little Port Sunlight Dock: regular cargo liner services, notably Blue Funnel and Nippon Line, used it to bring in a variety of raw materials which included copra, palm kernels, molasses, prepared vegetable oils, fats and whale oil. Outward bound were the products of the nearby factories, of which soap, margarine and cattle cake were probably the largest proportion. During World War 2 Bromborough Dock escaped damage in the Blitz, with the result that it was used for unloading large amounts of war supplies from America, and also for despatching to theatres of war the food and engineering products of the Lever companies.

The change for Bromborough Dock came in the 1960s, with a tendency for vegetable oils to be prepared in the country of origin: this led to a decline in tonnage and ultimately to the closure of the mills on the pool. Increasing worries about the possible extinction of the whale has led to a substitution of other oils, many of them home-produced; the boat traffic in oils between Bromborough and Crosfields Works at Warrington ceased in 1974, having outlasted the boats down from Weston Point (which used to lock out into the river at Weston Point, using the old

Right:
Lorries waiting at Brunswick Dock in 1962. Scenes like this are often taken as evidence of Liverpool's former prosperity; in fact they show the malaise of the old-style port. These lorries make money when they are moving, not when they are parked waiting for an archaic system of port operation to get round to accepting their goods. *MCM*

Below right:
In 1972 all the docks south of Pier Head were closed; in a rapidly changing world they were simply a vast liability. The grass grew on once-busy quays and the number of intact panes of glass in the windows steadily declined. Even the Albert warehouses — the largest 'first class listed' building in the country — decayed. Fortunately they were sufficiently well built to survive a decade of dereliction and remain restorable. *NWSIAH*

river channel rather than the Ship Canal) by only a few years.

Small-scale canal docks, such as those at Runcorn, Ellesmere Port and Weston Point, managed to hang on reasonably well for a while after World War 1, but the growth of road haulage and of the average size of ships was bound to tell in the end. In Runcorn, for example, the total tonnage passing through in 1952 was almost exactly one-tenth of the figure for 1884. The old line of locks was filled in during the 1950s, and in 1966 the new line, the Runcorn & Weston Canal and all the docks except Fenton, Alfred and the Tidal Dock followed. It was the end of the canal port, but not the end of Runcorn Docks. A similar process occurred at Ellesmere Port, with traffic dwindling during the 1930s and disappearing altogether in the late 1950s. The Shropshire Union Docks then lay entirely derelict until the arrival on the site of the Boat Museum in 1974. As at Runcorn, however, there was prosperity in a slightly different direction. Weston Point alone survived more or less as it had been. Traffic fell to about 30,000 tons in 1950 and once again the prophets of doom sharpened their pencils. Once again they were to be mistaken.

During the 1960s a number of factors came together to allow these small ports a new life. The larger, older ports like Liverpool were burdened with a past which made them expensive to operate. They had vast acreages of moribund undersized docks with huge sheds in poor states of repair, often with poor and outdated lifting appliances, some lacking even electric lighting. In short, their overheads were too high for them to be attractive to the smaller operator, and their wage bills and working practices were as obsolete as their premises. To a small port which could modernise relatively cheaply and quickly, rewards offered themselves. The revival can only be described as dramatic: the total of imports and exports at Runcorn rose from 44,110 tons in 1952 to 173,100 in 1962 and by 1972 to over half a million tons. At Weston Point, from the pitiable 30,000 tons in 1950 came again a result of about half a million in 1973.

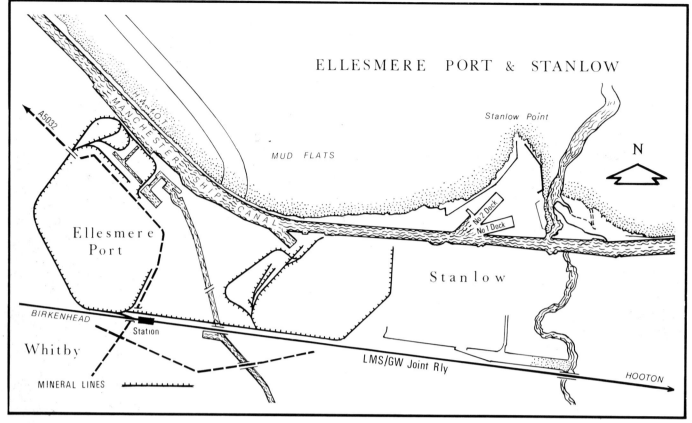

ELLESMERE PORT & STANLOW

Stanlow Point

MUD FLATS

No 2 Dock
No 1 Dock

Stanlow

N

Ellesmere
Port

BIRKENHEAD

Station

Whitby

MINERAL LINES

LMS/GW Joint Rly

HOOTON

Above:
Map of Ellesmere Port showing old canal docks and Stanlow.

Left:
The system became tidal, with the result that millions of cubic metres of silt found its way in, rendering the basins almost impossible either to use or to infill. Gaunt shells like that of the Piermaster's house littered the dockscape, and subsidence was affecting even the granite work of Hartley's masons. *NWSIAH*

The case at Ellesmere Port was rather different. There no revival of the old docks occurred, but the deep water berths on the North Quay provided a home for a new container depot in the 1970s. This, however, was not the crucial point, for the shipping interests of Ellesmere Port had long since undergone a dramatic change of direction.

A little way up the Ship Canal from the old docks, at Stanlow, was a convenient outcrop rock on the offshore side of the canal: it was an obviously promising site for a trade which the Ship Canal Co saw as having huge potential for growth, and which really needed to be located some way away from residential areas. In 1916 the company began to excavate the first Stanlow oil dock, which was completed in 1922, and followed by another larger one adjacent in 1933. In 1927 the channel of the canal was deepened from Eastham Locks through to Stanlow to allow access to ships of up to 15,000 tons. The new oil development was an outstanding success and Stanlow is still one of the major oil refining centres of the country. This upsurge of activities was followed by a number of private wharves on the Ship

Above:
Bromborough Pool, between Bromborough and Port Sunlight Docks. Abandoned on the mud lies the hull of a wooden Mersey flat, the once-universal estuarial small cargo vessel. *AEJ*

Left:
Bromborough Dock from the north, showing the berths and tanks for animal and vegetable oils — the raw materials for food and oleochemical industries nearby.
AEJ

Below:
One of the men who escaped from Sir Alfred Jones was the formidable William Lever; this is Port Sunlight Dock, an example of Lever's vertical integration in the soap industry. *AEJ*

Left:
Despite the growth in bulk and container cargoes, there was still work for the veteran *Mammoth*, seen here in steam at Gladstone Dock with a cargo of oil refinery equipment bound for Nigeria awaiting her attention. She was replaced by the new *Mersey Mammoth* in 1987. *AEJ*

Below left:
A superb early aerial view of Eastham Locks on the Manchester Ship Canal. In the distance, adjacent to the locks, is the hydraulic pumping station. The lofty sheerlegs in the foreground was for taking down and storing upper sections of mast or funnel which would not pass under the fixed bridges above Runcorn. Notice the paddle tug going furiously astern to slow the ship heading for the lock, and to compensate for a strong wind from starboard. *IAL*

Right:
The still-prosperous Queen Elizabeth II Dock dominates this more recent aerial view. The three different sizes of entrance lock for the canal still survive, but the little barge lock on the left is not used. *PoM*

Below right:
An aerial view of Garston Docks. The large dock in the foreground is Stalbridge, with Old Dock and New Dock beyond. The small dock in the foreground is the former graving dock of H. & C. Grayson, shipbuilders. The immense extent of the railway sidings is well shown, and seven of the eight coaling berths are occupied, although three of the wagon drops which were there in 1939 have been removed. In the right foreground, the industrial estate is still rail-connected. *IAL*

Canal, both for oil and for other products, including paper and motor cars. The headlong rush of the tanker trade into ever larger ships meant, however, that Stanlow Docks would be soon relegated to the second division and beyond, in a repetition of the movement downstream that we have seen elsewhere. The first step was the opening of the Queen Elizabeth II Dock at Eastham, just alongside the entrance locks of the Ship Canal, in January 1954. It was capable of handling the largest tankers then afloat, up to about 35,000dwt. It was connected by pipeline to Stanlow, but such was the headlong growth in tanker tonnage that its position in the front rank was not long retained, and the Tranmere oil berth, close to the old Rock Ferry Pier, capable of handling ships up to about 65,000dwt was opened in 1960. That too was rapidly outgrown, and the supertankers operated from a single buoy mooring off the tiny and obsolete port of Amlwch (Anglesey) where there was, in effect, no limit to the tonnage which could be handled. This process has now been reversed and crude arrives in vessels which enter the river.

At Ellesmere Port both the Port of Manchester's own general cargo traffic and Cawoods' container services are prospering, in 1987 container capacity was doubled to 100,000TEU per year. Fisher's operation at Manesty Wharf, despite being in competition with other services nearby, is also doing well, based on the facilities formerly used by the large Bowater paper mill.

Weston Point Docks, sadly, did not live up the promise shown in their astonishing revival in the 1960s and 1970s, and were now closed. Ocean Port Services re-opened trade there in 1986, with traffic in timber, scrap metal, steel and bulk cargoes. Runcorn is a different story, and a happier one because the general recession, whilst felt there, has not had any serious effect. Traffic was slack in 1982-83, falling off to about 300,000 tons, but has picked up again. The principal cargoes are dry bulk materials for the glass, pottery and fertiliser industries, but there is a significant trade in molten sulphur from Poland,

Below:

The port kept open during World War 2 with remarkable stamina, and the merchandise, whether food, industrial materials or weapons of war, kept flowing in. Here one of the Dock Board's floating cranes makes light work of lifting a Sherman tank. *MCM*

and Harker's tankers run up and down the Ship Canal and the river transferring small oil cargoes and providing bunkering services. The docks can accommodate ships carrying up to about 3,000 tons, but the sulphur is unloaded from the layby, where the limit is about 10,000 tons.

At Garston the story is a much happier one. In the 1950s Garston Docks appeared completely doomed, thanks to their principal association being with huge and obsolete railway installations. The hard times through which larger ports passed in the late 1960s changed all that for Garston as they did for other small ports, and it is now flourishing. At the time of writing, the entrance lock has been widened by nearly 50%, but this is only one of a series of measures to improve trade. The principal imports are now animal feeds, softwoods and steel, while there are cargo liner services to — among other places — Iceland, Yugoslavia, North America, Ireland and the Eastern Mediterranean.

Much of this traffic is, of course, in containers. The principal exports are what they always were: coal and salt. Large amounts of the latter go to Nigeria in 1-tonne bags, but the coal is mainly for the traditional markets in Ireland, Isle of Man and the Channel Islands. New coaling plant installed some six years ago may not look as impressive as the old LNWR wagon drops, but moves more than double the tonnage of coal with less breakage, less dust nuisance and less labour.

World War 2 placed Liverpool in an altogether unwanted position of prominence. The near-disaster of 1917, when unrestricted U-boat blockade had almost starved Britain, made it clear that the only adequate defence against submarines was the convoy system, and this was rapidly re-adopted after the outbreak of war in 1939. A convoy might consist of up to 50 or 60 ships, excluding the escorts, and many of them might arrive in need not only of docks and bunkering facilities but of repair work as well. The result was that convoyed shipping tended to be concentrated in major ports, and since the most numerous and important convoys were those from Canada and the USA, the ports of Bristol, Glasgow and Liverpool were by far the most important centres. With the new dimension of aerial bombardment this meant that the Port of Liverpool was very much in the front line.

The first casualty of the Blitz was a servant girl in Wirral, killed on 9 August 1940 when her employer's home was bombed, but the serious raids began in September when 221 people were killed in Liverpool. The intensity of raids varied, rising to a peak in December 1940 when deaths in Liverpool numbered 412, in Bootle 108, in Birkenhead 63 and in Wallasey 119. The worst damage to the port, and the heaviest casualties on the Liverpool side, were in the May Blitz of 1941 when 1,453 people were killed within the city alone. During the whole of the war no less than 91 ships were sunk in dock, and numerous dock buildings and installations were destroyed or damaged. The

Top right:

Near the end of steam haulage, a '9F' blasts out from the ore sidings at Bidston Dock on 20 October 1967, pulling about 1,000 tons of payload. The roaring safety valves betoken a determination to succeed on the long climb to Storeton Summit, where stalling point was often approached, and occasionally reached. *IAL*

Right:

A Russian RoRo vessel alongside the quay at Ellesmere Port. The container-size pallet in the right foreground is apt to illustrate how it has become worthwhile to render even classic break-bulk cargoes like bagged goods into unit loads. *PoM*

worst single incident was the loss of the Brocklebank liner *Malakand*, bombed in Huskisson Dock while still laden with a cargo which included over 1,000 tons of high explosive. The dock and its surrounding buildings were so devastated that no attempt was made to reinstate them after the war.

Railway yards and depots were frequently damaged, the Leeds & Liverpool Canal was breached, causing serious flooding, and huge areas of the industrial and commercial sectors of the city were completely flattened. In Liverpool the main weight of bombing ended with the May Blitz, but the weight of the attacks was the greatest outside of London. Some 120,000 houses were damaged and the number of homeless was at several times over 50,000 in Liverpool alone. This was the price of the port's astonishing ability to carry on business almost as usual. Despite the nightly chaos and destruction, 1,285 convoys arrived in the Mersey carrying some 70 million tons of cargo, with independent sailings bringing in about another 2,500,000 tons per year. Estimates of the number of troops passing through vary, but around 750,000 seems a fair guess from the sources available. Warships great and small, from the ubiquitous 'Flower' class corvettes of the convoy escorts to battleships, were bunkered or dry-docked, and of course added to by a remarkable output from Cammell Laird.

Despite the destruction achieved, the Mersey was no easy target for the Luftwaffe. There was heavy fighter protection from airfields all round the estuary, coupled with balloon barrages and a ferocious anti-aircraft (AA) box barrage over Cammell Laird. The raiders were getting towards the end of their fuel endurance and many met an unspectacular end by being chased west until they ran out of fuel. The Free Poles, flying Spitfires from Speke Airport, deposited much broken German machinery around Snowdonia. An unpleasant surprise for the raiders could often be found in the river, when to the land-based AA fire was added the armament of a 'Cairo' or a 'Black Swan' AA ship awaiting a convoy. A fairly well-documented tale is told of a 6in cruiser with a high-angle main armament caught in an air-raid, loosing 6in shells off furiously at raiders. A small administrative error in the magazines meant that one turret was supplied with armour-piercing shells for a time. These, of course, do not explode until they hit something, and what they hit was Parbold Hill, several miles northeast of Liverpool. As in other parts of the country, raiding did not cease through Goering's repentance of the evil, nor through a belief that the destruction was complete, but because the losses were becoming too high — Liverpool 1, Luftwaffe 0.

At sea the story was to be repeated. In the early months of the war, losses to U-boats were very heavy, so heavy that extrapolation of losses foretold starvation and the loss of the war. The reasons this did not happen were numerous and complex, but one of the more important ones may be singled out. This was the

Above:
Hauled by Type 4 (latterly Class 40) locomotive No D370, a cattle train crosses Morpeth Bridge on 21 August 1967, seen from the outward-bound side. Both the rolling lift bridge and the cattle train are characteristic of Birkenhead in the last years before the unit-loading revolution hit it. Morpeth Dock is now used for pleasure craft moorings and the occasional laid-up ferry boat. No cattle are imported, and most of the rails in this picture have been pulled up. *C. T. Gifford*

Top right:
The old coal drops on Old Dock, Garston, were nearing the end of their life when this picture was taken in the early 1970s. Notice how the coal descends from a great height, causing breakage and palls of dust. These were disadvantages which eventually outweighed the simplicity and low power requirement of the 19th century method. *AEJ*

Right:
A typical scene in the modern Port of Liverpool: the Royal Seaforth Dock is the flag-bearer of the system, capable of handling the largest container ships with ease. Container ships and the equipment for loading and offloading may not be beautiful, but they are highly effective in the vital business of reducing the turnaround time. *MD&HC*

matter of escort tactics and training, which was crucial if escorts were to be able both to detach from the convoy to counter-attack and to continue to screen the convoy while this was going on. The answer was found in Liverpool, by Sir Percy Noble and his successor Sir Max Horton, of Western Approaches Command. In consultation with the acknowledged 'aces' of U-boat hunting and killing, men like Lt-Cdr Peter Gretton and the legendary Capt 'Johnny' Walker, they produced simple guidelines and procedures which could be carried out even in the hideously confusing circumstances of a night attack on a convoy. Above all, escort groups were to be specifically trained for the job and then kept together as teams. Shipboard training was carried out at HMS *Tobermory* (Isle of Mull) while the endless drilling and practice of depth charge handling and action procedures took place in Liverpool Docks. By the end of 1941 the U-boats were paying a higher price for their attacks on merchantmen, and by late 1943 the price had risen to the point where they were defeated. That defeat was largely planned and managed from a basement in Chapel Street, Liverpool. The port remained open and through it flowed the materials for victory.

That victory saw a daunting problem of reconstruction. Instead of the port being able to plan ahead, it had to spend the next few years 'running to standstill' in order merely to get itself back to the state in which it had been in 1939. In some cases reinstatement could incorporate modernisation, but money for large-scale improvements to entrances, for example, was hard to find. Rebuilding damaged sheds was scarcely going to shape a new future for the port.

Soon after the end of World War 2 a number of things started to go wrong for Liverpool, as for many other larger, older ports. Some of the primary commodities which used to be imported in large quantities — such as cotton or palm kernels — began to be processed in their country of origin. If the resulting product came here at all, it did so at least part-finished and therefore weighing much less. These and other developments also damaged some of the port's biggest users on the export side — again cotton was the most notable example. At the same time, the port had to face the loss of traditional 'Imperial' markets through shifts in international politics, and it had internal problems of its own. Much of its plant and many of its quayside buildings were getting old: new investment had been hard to make during the depressed 1930s and the war, while the period immediately after the war had been mostly occupied with making good war damage.

The full employment of the 'You've never had it so good' era did not help

Above:
Whilst some of the container ships are owned by firms with long Liverpool connections (ACL for example is a consortium which includes Cunard-Brocklebank) there are many visitors from other countries, often flying flags of convenience. *MD&HC*

either: if the port found it difficult to invest in new plant, it also found it hard to meet the rising labour costs of operating in the old-fashioned way. Disputes proliferated and got the port an evil reputation which it has taken many years to dispel. At the same time that this was happening the size of ships was rising rapidly, and the near-disappearance of Liverpool's bread and butter for the past century, the general cargo liner, became a foreseeable possibility. The reason for this was the appearance of the new generation of cargo vessels, which saw nearly all types of cargo fall into one of three categories: bulk, roll-on/roll-off (RoRo) or containerised. None of these required what Liverpool had most of: miles of quaysides on spine-and-branch docks, with miles of transit sheds. They required a few very large specialised berths with lots of open space around them, good connections with motorways and main line railways, and almost nothing else. It was a question of adapt — or die.

Adaptation was not avoided. Some trades had already gone into bulk transit in a big way, including grain and sugar: the problem was that these facilities, too, had

been left behind for they were at docks like Brunswick and Huskisson which could no longer take large enough ships. It became clear that what was needed did not fall far short of building a new port. Of what there was, only a small part of the northernmost docks would be large enough, and easy enough of access to see out the revolution which had already started. The first container berth opened at Gladstone in 1969, by which time construction work was well under way immediately to the north where the Royal Seaforth Dock would be completed by 1972. At the same time, liabilities were being shed: all docks upstream of Pierhead closed in 1972 and the Dock Railway followed in 1973. The Central Docks came to be used less and less, and the docks on the Birkenhead side also suffered some diminution of traffic.

At Seaforth the facilities are matched to the market for large amounts of goods in a few very large ships (Atlantic Container Line's latest vessels carry 45,000 tonnes of goods). Three mills, whose silos are visible for miles, mark the grain terminal which has a deepwater berth and one smaller one for transhipment cargoes. It was recently announced that further investment is to take place. Cargoes are both for human consumption and in the growing trade in imported animal feeds. There are four container berths, two of which also have RoRo facilities, and a large terminal for timber and timber products. Almost every country which used to be served by the

Above:
Liverpool has always been an important centre for timber imports, and this busy scene is at the Royal Seaforth timber terminal. In the left background are the container berths and to the right the grain terminal; beyond lie Gladstone and Hornby Docks. *MD&HC*

Below:
The pace of industrial change and the decline in output in the British steel industry have increased the supply of scrap at the same time as reducing the domestic demand. Garston, like Liverpool, has not been slow to profit from this trend by running a thriving trade in scrap exports. *AEJ*

dozens of cargo liner companies with their hundreds of appropriated berths is represented here to some extent, though many of the ships providing those services now sail under the flags of what would once have been highly improbable nations. A slightly sad trade, perhaps, but one in which Liverpool has gained a good deal of traffic is that in scrap metal. There is a berth at Seaforth for the really large shipments, and seven other berths are in use for this trade, which now amounts to about 700,000+ tons per year.

There are many developments which can affect a port's fortunes whilst remaining utterly beyond its control. Britain's joining the EEC did not do traffic through Liverpool any good at all: in particular it was the direct cause of its losing most of its sugar traffic from the West Indies, but more generally it has resulted in a shift in emphasis from the Atlantic to the North Sea. The Falklands War resulted in a serious loss of traffic with the East Coast of South America, one of Liverpool's traditional trading strongholds, by no means all of which has yet been recovered. On the credit side, and probably the most hopeful development since the opening of Royal Seaforth, is Liverpool's new status as a Freeport. The area bounded by the Freeport security system is not, for Customs purposes, considered as UK territory. Neither duties nor VAT are payable on goods so long as they remain therein: if they pass into Britain or any other EEC country duty and VAT become payable, as do EEC levies. If goods are re-exported to non-EEC countries they remain duty-free. For the customer this gives considerable cash-flow advantages, and to the Mersey Docks & Harbour Co it offers a great saving in administrative costs which is shared by and with the customer.

The policy of centralising activities at the north end continues. The Irish Ferry services have moved from Waterloo up to Langton Dock, but the docks immediately to the south of the Freeport have recently experienced a growth of traffic in scrap metal and general cargo. North of that point a great deal of activity is evident, but because relatively few people pass by that way, and ships no longer come up the river, many people fail to realise what is going on. The Mersey has had its ups and downs over the centuries, and the last 20 years have been particularly fraught with difficulties and the need for rapid and radical change. There have been many casualties and there could possibly be one or two more — during the writing of this book, the closure of Bromborough Dock was announced, completely out of the blue. On the other hand new traffic, such as bulk solids wharfs at Gladstone and the twice-daily Dublin Ro-Ro service operated by Pandora, have been found. It appears that Liverpool, Garston and the lower

Above:
The container berths at Garston are usually busy, and the throughput of containers is growing with continuing investment. Although this view gives the impression that the operation is road-based, there is also a major Freightliner terminal. Some transfer of containers to and from Royal Seaforth takes place, but this is mainly by road. AEJ

Below:
New coal loaders at Garston in action: the loading chute is controlled from the cab above the quayside and can be moved around the hold to trim the cargo by one man from that position. There is a conspicuous absence of the clouds of coal dust which used to accompany the loading of coal by traditional methods. AEJ

reaches of the Ship Canal have weathered the storm, and may now hope to reap the benefits. The record of the Mersey ports in facing, for example, the cotton famine of the American Civil War or the Blitz suggests that their resilience is more than adequate.

The Future of Merseyside and its Ports

One 'resource' of which Merseyside has long had in plenty is the prophets of doom, and over the last decade they have had a marvellous time as one blow after another damaged the foundations of Liverpool's trade and the associated industry in the immediate area. If we are to make even remotely intelligent guesses as to the future of trade on and about the Mersey it will be necessary to pick out a few of the trends and events which have caused decline.

The first, and possibly most important, of these was the dependence of Liverpool on old-established industries which were in turn geared to a colonial market, especially heavy engineering and shipbuilding, and those which depended merely on traditional supremacy unsupported by progressive improvement in efficiency, such as cotton. Industries such as these were bound to crumble as ex-colonial nations became cheap labour areas in competition with their former colonial masters. Behind this, however, lay something more fundamental: Liverpool had, for example, survived the abolition of the slave trade with its potentially disastrous effects, by its once traditional spirit of enterprise: in the days of its growth Liverpool did not jump on bandwagons, it was already aboard them when they were built. The ability to spot and invest in the next boom trade seemed to desert the port.

Overpopulation, or rather the unfounded worry of it, was another major destroyer. Before World War 2, Liverpool was already exporting people outside of its own boundaries. This was done from the best of motives — to release people from often disgusting overcrowding in the city

Above right:
The Royal Navy have long been welcome visitors in the Mersey (at least since impressment ended they have been!). The crew of HMS *Albion* line the flightdeck as she approaches the stage in May 1967. The stage hands have seen it all before. *MCM*

Right:
Despite all the doom and gloom which passes for description of Liverpool, it is still the largest export port in Britain. The Carline service provides a roll-on/roll-off service to Eire for Ford cars from the Halewood Works, carrying an average of 200 vehicles per trip. *MD&HC*

centre. The unfortunate consequence was a diminution of the rate base, meaning that the costs of local government fell on ever fewer people and businesses. The people who moved out tended to be the younger and more productive ones, which meant that the revenue diminished more than did the demand for services. Whilst this was scarcely a serious problem in the late 1930s it had become so by the 1960s, and Liverpool was still busily exporting people then, when the overpopulation problem was demonstrably mythical.

Central government made its contribution to the problem by encouraging the development of New Towns. Whatever may be said in favour of New Towns, there can be little doubt that they have been responsible for serious damage to Merseyside and other older conurbations. They have take industry into the countryside,

Above:
This photograph, with the following one, shows a transformation perhaps even more remarkable than the modernisation of the north end of the port. In the left foreground is Herculaneum Dock, many feet deep in shifting silt which generated methane; the dry docks have been partly filled with rubbish. In the centre are the unlovely remains of the Dingle oil terminal, with rotting jetties, remains of underground tanks and a dubious river wall. *MDC*

Right:
A little over two years later, the International Garden Festival is open. Some features of the old dock have been retained, but the silt has gone in favour of a load-bearing fill and the oil terminal has been landscaped with striking rapidity. To assess the value of the venture, one need look no further than the number of parked cars. *MDC*

leaving a desert in the cities. Despite the money which government now puts into the special development areas, it continues to encourage the development of these economic leeches feeding on the blood of the older industrial areas.

Finally, it is worth mentioning that Merseyside has suffered more than most areas from the attention of the news media. It has acquired a truly atrocious public image, some of which is long out of date, and much of which was not true to start with. Not only do the press and television seem to go to a great deal of trouble to find unpleasant stories about

Merseyside, they are not necessarily truthful. For example, a particularly bitter industrial dispute involving a printing works in Warrington was adjusted to fit the preconceptions of Merseyside in a very simple manner. Warrington is in Cheshire, a nice genteel shire county, and everyone knows that Liverpool has the most awkward bloody-minded workers in the whole world. The answer adopted by the Media was direct and to the point: it lied

about the location of Warrington. The result of this kind of smear campaign is a shortage of new investment and, one has to admit, a tendency among some of the more anti-social local inhabitants to live up to what they read about themselves.

And so to the crystal ball. The problem of population loss took a long time in being recognised, but is now well known. Some attempts at remedial action are showing fruit, especially with reference to the construction of new housing both for sale and for rent in the older urban areas. Of course it is too late in coming, but there are grounds for hoping that this particular manifestation of decay is being tackled with some modest success. If it works it will bring more money into the local economy, whereupon the multiplier effect (in the inexact sense) will begin to work. The city (and the region) may depend very heavily on the trade of the river, but the trade depends on a strong local economic infrastructure. Sadly there does not seem to be much sign of Central Government tackling its side of the problem: no amount of cosmetic tree-planting exercises can camouflage the fact that successive governments have followed policies which favour greenfield development, and those prefer-

Below:
Leinster and **Connaught** lack the looks of the first **Mauretania**, but there is still a certain elegance to a passenger ship which even modern ideas of cost-effectiveness (to say nothing of ugly smoke deflectors) cannot entirely remove. *B&I*

ably south of Birmingham. Recent announcements relating to London getting yet another airport and the North of England not getting a chance of staging the Olympic Games can scarcely have been seen as favourable pointers.

The public image shows little sign of improvement, but there are some seeds of hope. More 'good' stories seem to be emerging, mostly in connection with the activities of the Merseyside Development Corporation. The humble beginnings of this are to be seen in the growth of the local tourist industry, which may seem peripheral: it is not peripheral, for visitors to the area almost invariably go away quite surprised at how much better it was than they expected. Among them are potential investors. The money they spend on goods and services on their visit helps the local economy, but that is almost peripheral.

There remains the key question: can the area survive the decline in its old traditional trades? The signs are that it is beginning to find the way, with the establishment of new high technology industries. Nor should we forget the 'hungriest' section of local industry, which is made up of small (sometimes tiny) firms which have grown from the ruins of larger and older ones, often capitalised on redundancy payments. If one or two outstanding success stories could become more typical, the salvation of the local economy could well lie there. Goods in and out of the Mersey are the basic necessity, and the better the local manufacturing and

service base the more likely it is that the quantity will rise. The indications on the rapidly reviving former dockland under the control of the Merseyside Development Corporation are that new investment is not quite as scarce as it was, and that some of that old spirit of enterprise which made Liverpool a great port is once again to be seen in the smaller undertakings.

The Port of Liverpool, it seems, has already dragged itself up from the morbid condition to which it had sunk in the 1960s, and the greater part of the smaller dock undertakings around the estuary have success stories of their own, Garston being perhaps the most impressive. Liverpool's new Freeport status could well prove to be a vital contribution to the revival of some traditional process industries. What appears to be missing is the interaction between the port and the rest of the local economy which was at the heart of the spiralling growth of the 19th century. The signs of an upturn in the local economy show some promise that Liverpool may once again 'get its act together', re-establishing the river, its docks and its trade as the unifying factor of a substantial and potentially hugely prosperous area. Merseyside should not need to wait for the day when oil prices rise to the point where the oil in Liverpool Bay is worth extracting: before then it should have started on the rising spiral and, like Felixstowe, realised the truth of the words of the economist who said 'To him that hath, more shall be given'.

An Architectural Digression

The buildings of the Dock Estate in Liverpool show two main themes: rugged functional simplicity as in the Albert Dock warehouses and commercial bravado designed to emphasise the wealth and power of the port, as in the case of the Albert Dock Traffic Office. Almost every building dating from before World War 1 has the equally recognisable sub-theme that it was intended to fulfil its function or impress the onlooker for a very long time indeed. Jesse Hartley was described at the time as 'building for posterity', and the way in which his buildings have survived is ample proof of the quality of his work. Nor should we forget that Hartley was only the most spectacular and prolific of the builders of dockside buildings: other architects and engineers followed similar guidelines with results which are distinctive in their style but identical in their basic philosophy.

The quest for durability, combined with the sheer size of many of the buildings, was bound to make an impact on the overall townscape of Liverpool. Because the shipping industry was so dominant, and because its dominance lasted through more than a century of intensive building, the effect goes further than that. Shipping men and shipping money determined the whole appearance of the area to an extent at least as great as that to which cotton moulded large parts of Lancashire. Seven miles of waterfront were denied to the local population, occupied by docks and their associated storage and service buildings. Only at Pierhead could Merseysiders

Above right:
Hartley's dour nature did not restrict him to a prosaic style of building, as this astonishing pumping station at Canada Entrance (1859) shows. The characteristic 'Cyclopean Granite' masonry is evident on the river wall, but it is the huge accumulator tower which overpowers all else. *MCM*

Right:
G. F. Lyster, successor to Hartley was not exactly self-effacing when it came to building pumping stations either. This wonderful piece of fantasy stood (part of it still stands) at Langton Graving Dock, providing both pump-out for the dock and hydraulic power. *MCM*

indulge their liking for watching ships come and go, unless they were to travel some considerable distance. Their willingness to do this led to the appearance of buildings to serve those ferry routes which were pleasure-orientated, like the Eastham Ferry Hotel or, later on, a large proportion of New Brighton.

We can however spread the net much wider, and probably should. Some of the most spectacular buildings in the centre of Liverpool are shipping offices, including the Cunard building and the enormous India buildings. The former White Star building always calls to mind the style of New Scotland Yard, which is scarcely surprising, as both were designed by Norman Shaw. Begun in that same year of 1897, by the same architect, is another of Liverpool's gems, the Royal Insurance building in North John Street. Inseparable from the functions of the docks themselves, and of the shipping offices which depended upon them, was the work of the insurers, whose financial back-up was an essential part of Liverpool's trade. This connection still exists, as the new Royal Insurance building in Old Hall Street demonstrates. Not to everybody's taste architecturally, and often rudely known as 'the sand castle', it nonetheless emphasises, just by its towering bulk, that there is more to a great port than a lot of docks and cranes.

May one go further? Liverpool is rich in civic and institutional buildings, of which the Town Hall and St George's Hall are just the two most obvious. On a smaller scale, Birkenhead, Bootle and Wallasey each have buildings of some pretension, and considerable merit. If we compare the institutional buildings of different towns, it is obvious that they tend to reflect both in quality and quantity, the period when the town was best able to afford to build non-essentials. In short, Liverpool's heritage has been largely moulded by the existence of large amounts of disposable money during the last two-thirds of last century — the rewards of the docks and their trade. The establishment and/or endowment of any new charitable or cultural initiative was almost invariably connected with the shipping interest, though one must always remember the occasional exception like Sir Andrew Barclay Walker, the brewer who gave Liverpool its art gallery. In some cases, like that of the celebrated Sailor's Home, a victim of the development fever of the 1970s, the connection was obvious and even the location was close to the docks which called them forth. In others the visitor must look on brass plates for the names of benefactors — names which often include Holt or Rathbone, Gladstone or Ismay.

In the same way that Liverpool's institutional buildings reflect the period of the greatest prosperity of the port, so too do its churches. Being an international city, Liverpool's churches had an international flavour, catering not only for a Catholic population of much above average size, but also for Greeks and Russians, Swedes and Norwegians, Welsh and Scottish. Generosity to the church was a recognised virtue in late 19th century England, so it will come as no surprise that we find large gifts and endowments to splendid churches of all denominations. Sadly, a decline in church-going and in the population of Liverpool has thinned the ranks of these buildings, but many still remain. St Agnes, Ullet Road, in the heart of an area of wealthy merchant homes, is a good example. Beautifully built and richly furnished and appointed, it was paid for by just one wealthy local resident. The supreme monument to the piety of the shipping classes, however, towering both literally and metaphorically over everything else, is Liverpool Cathedral. Superlatives surround the largest Anglican church in the world, the largest cathedral in England, with the largest organ in Britain, the highest and heaviest ringing peal of bells in Europe — and the richest shipping magnates to get its building fund away to a good start. The bells, for example, together with the 330ft tower in which they hang, were paid for with a gift of over £225,000 from the Vestey family.

Two Liverpool churches have an unusual and much more direct connection with the port. St George's Everton and St Michael in the Hamlet were completed in 1814 and 1815 respectively with their structures entirely of iron. The parts were cast in John Cragg's ironworks in central Liverpool to the designs of Thomas Rickman, and their connection with the port was that they were envisaged as prototypes for modular construction churches for export to the colonies. The expanses of brickwork visible are only there to keep out the weather — the ironwork fulfils all the structural functions, and they are therefore suitable for erection by a workforce of relatively limited skills. In the event no churches of such size were exported, but Liverpool did corner the market in smaller build-it-yourself church

kits of the type usually and irreverently known as 'tin tabernacles', with no less than four local firms exporting them all over the world. (An example by Isaac Dixon is still to be seen at Hassall Green in darkest Staffordshire.)

We cannot really close a section on the buildings which grew up around and because of the docks of Liverpool without looking briefly at housing. Most of the history of working-class housing in and around the dockside area has been obscured through the well intentioned hooliganism of planners and politicians in the 1950s and 1960s.

The consequences of their naïve assumption that property could not be improved — that the only answer to substandard housing is demolition — have been horrifying, not only in historical terms but in the social, financial and environmental consequences. In the process of playing the role of Corbusier and/or God, they destroyed buildings and communities alike, things they could not begin to understand, let alone rebuild. The sad result is that the only evidence we have for most of the working-class housing of the late 19th century is that which was collected when it had deteriorated to the point where someone wanted to pull it down, and took a photograph — carefully framed — to show that the property

needed to be pulled down. Only the houses of a small minority of port workers — the elite craftsmen who lived in the new pressed-brick terraces of the 1890-1914 period — have survived in any numbers and in something like their original form.

The houses of the great shipowners have suffered almost as much: built when labour for running and maintenance was cheap,

they have largely disappeared when these conditions no longer obtained. In the beginning, the shipowners lived in the town centre, at the heart of their own trade. Later, as in other cities, increasing density of population and the absence of effective sewage pumping systems caused them to move uphill, a tendency reflected in a well known local schoolboy's parody

beginning 'The sewage in the Mersey is not strained . . .' Of these first two phases, only a handful of barely recognisable examples survives: the few good examples of shipowners' houses we can find mainly belong to the third stage, the move to the suburbs. This occurred at two levels: some shipowners, like the Holts, built their principal home on the outskirts of the port, while others maintained a country house in imitation of the aristocracy, confining their Liverpool property to a grandiose flat in which some entertaining could be undertaken. The Larrinaga family recently disposed of a fine example of the latter type. The style of shipowner's property which we think of as being characteristic is the 'pocket country estate', a house capable of fulfilling the social role of an aristocratic household, but standing in perhaps 50 acres. A surprisingly large number of these establishments existed on the fringes of the port, of which Sudley and Greenbank survive in a form sufficiently complete to allow imagination to make up the deficiencies, while a couple of others require rather more imagination.

The area in between is where the bulk of survivals lie. Houses built between about 1840 and 1914 of roughly 6-10 bedrooms and varying degrees of gentility are still very much in use (especially by the author, who lives in one) but can scarcely be described as necessarily connected with the port. Of course the people who built them often lived on the proceeds of shipping, but the direct connection of the workers at one end and the owners at the other is absent.

The possible extensions of the story of Liverpool and its ports are, like the wealth of Lever, almost literally boundless, and we must stop somewhere. Perhaps we may leave the line hazy, remembering that Liverpool sat at the crossroads of the greatest trading empire the world had ever seen, and that the wealth of that trade could scarcely fail to be reflected in the local building fabric. We may also, perhaps, be allowed a little regret that the supremely cheap and nasty years of the 1960s and 1970s have managed to pawn our inheritance without getting much for it.

Above right:
There is still a rich profusion of assorted Police huts and gate houses around the older parts of the docks. Some are in cyclopean granite, others in dressed granite, but even the plain cheap brick ones are of great quality compared with anything which could be constructed now for such a modest purpose. Overspecified they may have been, but they have certainly proved durable. *AEJ*

Right:
Typical of the 'pocket stately homes' built by the Liverpool shipping magnates is Sudley, once the property of the Holt family, and now a branch of the National Museums & Galleries on Merseyside. *AEJ*

Bibliography

Docks of the Mersey: A Short Critical Bibliography

General works

History of Liverpool: Ramsay Muir (1907, reprinted 1970 by SR). Written for the celebrations of the 700th anniversary of King John's Charter, it is still the best general account of the earlier history of the town and port, although a little thin on industry and transport.

A Merseyside Town in the Industrial Revolution: T. C. Barker & J. R. Harris (1959, Casson). A new edition is rumoured. This book is primarily about St Helens, but its broad scope gives excellent sidelights on Widnes, Garston, Liverpool and the Weaver. A classic work which set new standards in local history.

Birkenhead 1877-1974: Myrra Lee (1974, County Borough of Birkenhead). Really an obsequy for the independent borough and a history of the municipality, it nevertheless has much to offer as a general account of an important town whose history is underpublished.

A History of Runcorn: C. Nickson (1887, Mackie). Whilst a number of books give some account of Runcorn from one or other specialist point of view, it is nearly a century since anyone wrote a general work.

A Guide to Merseyside's Industrial Past: Paul Rees (1984, NWSIAH). An excellent short gazetteer to the sites of industrial interest in Merseyside. Since so much of Merseyside's past is transport-orientated, the majority of the entries relate in one way or another to the port. Enables speedy location of interesting buildings.

Books about ports

Liverpool and the Mersey: F. E. Hyde (1971, David & Charles). If one had to recommend only one book on the history of the Port of Liverpool, this would have to be the one. Necessarily brief in places, but its breadth of coverage is superb.

Western Gateway: S. Mountfield (MD&HB). A detailed history of the Dock Board and its antecedents. Written from the 'inside', with both advantages and disadvantages which that implies.

Business in Great Waters: MD&HB (1958, Newman Neame). A short centenary history of the Dock Board. Easy to digest and very well illustrated. It is perhaps as useful for what it tells us about the Dock Board at the time of writing as for its coverage of the previous century.

Jesse Hartley, Dock Engineer: Nancy Ritchie-Noakes (1980, Merseyside County Museums). A small picture history of a great man. Many interesting insights and excellent illustrations which help to correct a century or so of neglect of Hartley.

Liverpool's Historic Waterfront: Nancy Ritchie-Noakes (1984, HMSO). An expensive publication, and that is about all that can be said against it. Solidly based on a great deal of research into the paperwork and fabric of the port alike.

Ellesmere Port — Canal Town: Adrian Jarvis (1977, Boat Museum/Avon Anglia). A concise description of the growth of Ellesmere Port docks and their trade between 1795 and 1921.

Canal Ports: J. Douglas Porteous (1977, Academic Press). A substantial study of the development of canal ports in general. Two of the case studies chosen are Ellesmere Port and Runcorn, with valuable sections on each.

Schooner Port: Two Centuries of Upper Mersey Sail: H. S. Starkey (1983 G. W. & A. Hesketh).

Books about related topics

Liverpool Transport: J. B. Horne and T. B. Manud (1982, Transport Publishing). (Two volumes, a third in preparation.) Compendious account of buses and trams in Liverpool from the early horsebus operators to (presently) 1930. Minutely researched and well illustrated.

Roads, Rails and Ferries of Liverpool: J. Joyce (1983, Ian Allan Ltd). Broad-ranging account of developments which, whilst not directly connected with the docks, are inseparable from them. The best general guide to the infrastructure of local transport.

The Liverpool Overhead Railway: C. E. Box, revised A. Jarvis (1984, Ian Allan Ltd). Authoritative account of a pioneering little railway which was built to serve the docks. Many points of interaction, and many good illustrations, the majority of them taken by Box himself, taking advantage of his privileged position as 'the Boss's son'.